The *OBSCURE* Bible Study Series – Book 6 Personal Study Guide

Why is this Book Cover Different?

This is one of three books on which we have recently
changed the covers in order to promote
the concept that this
Bible Study Series is about:

The Intriguing Lives of Obscure Bible Characters!

Unfortunately our initial covers didn't send
this message, so we are experimenting
to see if these new covers do send
the right message about these books.

The OBSCURE BIBLE STUDY SERIES is a 9 book series
based on unique, uncommon, and even obscure
Bible characters and events.

The *OBSCURE* Bible Study Series – Book 6 Personal Study Guide

"Wisdom That Transforms. Action That Lasts."

The Get Wisdom Commitment

At Get Wisdom Publishing we believe that true wisdom has the power to transform lives. Our mission is to equip readers with timeless insights and practical tools that inspire growth, guide decisions, and empower purposeful living. We don't just inform—we empower.

Our books combine profound understanding with real-life application, enabling readers to unlock their potential and navigate life's challenges with clarity and confidence. With each step guided by wisdom, we help you create lasting change and live the life you deserve.

When wisdom meets purpose, transformation follows.

The *OBSCURE* Bible Study Series – Book 6 Personal Study Guide

The *OBSCURE* Bible Study Series

Grow in your faith through investigating unusual and obscure biblical characters.

"Deep Biblical Wisdom. Real-Life Faith Application."

The OBSCURE Bible Study Journey

Meet Shamgar, Jethro, Manoah & Hathach	4 Lessons
Blasphemy, Grace, Quarrels & Reconciliation	8 Lessons
The Beginning and the End	8 Lessons
God at the Center	8 Lessons
Women of Courage	8 Lessons
The Beginning of Wisdom	8 Lessons
Miracles and Rebellion	8 Lessons
The Chosen People	8 Lessons
The Chosen Person	8 Lessons

The *OBSCURE* Bible Study Series – Book 6 Personal Study Guide

The Beginning of Wisdom

Your personal character counts!

Personal Study Guide
Book 6

*Experience the transformative power
of biblical wisdom.*

Stephen H Berkey

The *OBSCURE* Bible Study Series – Book 6 Personal Study Guide

COPYRIGHT

The Beginning if Wisdom: Your personal character counts, by Stephen H Berkey. Published by Get Wisdom Publishing, 1810 Bittersweet Trail, Thompsons Station, TN 37179. Copyright © 2020 Stephen H Berkey. www.getwisdompublishing.com

All rights reserved. No portion of this book may be reproduced in any form without written permission from the publisher, except as permitted by U.S. copyright law. For permission contact: info@getwisdompublishing.com

ISBN 978-1-952359-10-1   (Leader Guide, paperback)

ISBN 978-1-952359-11-8   (Leader Guide, ebook)

ISBN 978-1-952359-12-5   (Personal Study Guide, paperback)

ISBN 978-1-952359-13-2   (Personal Study Guide, ebook)

Audiobook available   (amazon.com and audible.com)

Bible Translations Used:

Unmarked scriptures and scriptures marked ESV are taken from THE HOLY BIBLE, ENGLISH STANDARD VERSION (ESV): Scriptures taken from THE HOLY BIBLE, ENGLISH STANDARD VERSION ® Copyright© 2001 by Crossway, a publishing ministry of Good News Publishers. Used by permission.

Scriptures marked NIV are taken from the NEW INTERNATIONAL VERSION (NIV): Scripture taken from THE HOLY BIBLE, NEW INTERNATIONAL VERSION ®. Copyright© 1973, 1978, 1984, 2011 by Biblica, Inc.™. Used by permission of Zondervan.

Scriptures marked HCSB are taken from the HOLMAN CHRISTIAN STANDARD BIBLE (HCSB): Scripture taken from the HOLMAN CHRISTIAN STANDARD BIBLE, copyright© 1999, 2000, 2002, 2003 by Holman Bible Publishers, Nashville Tennessee. All rights reserved.

Discover the biblical characters that mainstream studies forget – and the timeless lessons they teach."

The **OBSCURE** Bible Study Series – Book 6 Personal Study Guide

TABLE OF CONTENTS

Title Pages ii
Copyright iv
Table of Contents v
Free Resources vi
Why Study OBSCURE Characters? viii
About The Leader Guide ix
Book Description x
Introduction xii

Transformation Roadmap 108
Free PDF Resources 109
Next Steps 111
The OBSCURE Series 112
The Jesus Follower Series 113
The Life Planning Series 114
Prayer Guide 115
Acknowledgments 116
Notes 117
About the Author 118
Contact Us 119

CONTENTS

The Hypocrites, the Pharisees 01

Benaiah, killed a lion in a pit 13

the Ten Lepers, Jesus healed 25

Stephen, stoned to death 37

Demas, he deserted Paul 51

Onesimus, a slave of Philemon 64

Rabshakeh, title of Assyrian official 76

Elihu, Job's young protagonist 94

The *OBSCURE* Bible Study Series – Book 6 Personal Study Guide

FREE PDF RESOURCES

Living Wisely
The Life Planning Guide

> *A Quick-Start Guide to Purposeful Living and Wise Decisions!*
>
> Discover the five life domains: purpose, people, principles, productivity, and perspective. Wisdom is the ability to apply truth and logic to real-life decisions and produce good outcomes. It influences your choices and will produce action that lasts. Consider and apply the five practical wisdom principles for daily living. (6 pages)
>
> **Free PDF:** https://getwisdompublishing.com/resource-registration/

Free PDF

Five Practical Principles For Life

When wisdom meets purpose, transformation follows.

The *OBSCURE* Bible Study Series – Book 6 Personal Study Guide

Free PDF
Wise Decision-Making

[Get the ebook version for 99 cents]

> ### *You can make good choices.*
>
> **This free resource provides a project-oriented perspective and gives ten detailed steps to analyze issues/problems to determine a solution.** (26 pages)
>
> Good decisions expand your horizons. Don't allow the fear of decision-making paralyze your ability to make good choices. Think through the reasonable alternatives and move forward. When your eyes are on the goal, making good decisions is easier.
>
> **Free PDF:** https://getwisdompublishing.com/resource-registration/
>
> **Kindle ebook for 99 cents:** https://www.amazon.com/dp/B09SYGWRVL/

Ebook

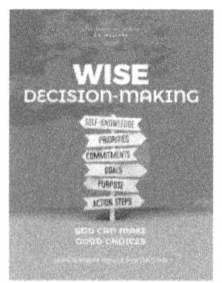

Free PDF

Make Thoughtful Decisions!

Good decisions expand your horizons.

The *OBSCURE* Bible Study Series – Book 6 Personal Study Guide

Why Study OBSCURE Characters?

Unique, New, and Fresh
For experienced Bible students these characters will provide a fresh and interesting approach to Bible study. Since most of the material will be unfamiliar to the participants, new believers or those just starting Bible study should not feel intimidated by students who have been studying for years. Most readers will not be acquainted with the majority of the characters and events in this series.

Knowledge of Scripture
These studies are a great introduction for those just beginning Bible study. Regardless of their level of knowledge, everyone should find the characters and stories provide an opportunity to grow in their faith through investigating fascinating and unusual biblical stories and incidents.

Valuable Life Lessons
These lesser-known characters are a lot like you and me. God uses all sorts of people to accomplish His plans! You will become familiar with ordinary people, strange characters, and people living on the fringe of life who have the same troubles and challenges as people today. The deep truths and life lessons embedded in these studies should be valuable. They will provide new insights to scripture.

*"Unlock Biblical Wisdom.
Transform Your faith!"*

The *OBSCURE* Bible Study Series – Book 6 Personal Study Guide

ABOUT THE LEADER GUIDE

All of the books in this Bible Study series have an extensive Leader Guide. If you are a participant in a group, a Leader Guide is not necessary, unless you want the author's answers. If you are studying independently, you may want the Leader Guide.

In the Guide the answers follow the questions with a small amount of space for the Leader's personal responses. If you are using the Leader Guide and want to do the study without the influence of the author's answers the best solution is to obtain the blank Worksheets, which are free. This will allow you to record your answers separately before reviewing the answers in the Leader Guide.

See the instructions on the previous "FREE RESOURCES" page to access the free Worksheets.

"Discover the Overlooked.
Apply it to Your Life!"

The *OBSCURE* Bible Study Series – Book 6 Personal Study Guide

Book Description

Equip Yourself for Life's Battles: Timeless Wisdom from Biblical Underdogs

Are you seeking a life of purpose and fulfillment, yet feeling stagnant in your spiritual growth? Do you long to live out your faith authentically, but often stumble and feel like you're falling short?

This study equips you with the essential tools to navigate life's challenges and cultivate a character that pleases God. Delve into the stories of hypocritical Pharisees, the lepers who rejected God, and stand alongside David as he fought through great adversity. Through focused biblical wisdom and actionable insights, this Get Wisdom Publishing study will guide you towards a deeper, more meaningful faith. This isn't just another read; you will move from knowing about, to being about.

Learn to recognize and overcome hypocrisy in your own life. Embrace courage and loyalty like Benaiah, the fearless warrior. Cultivate gratitude like the one leper who returned to thank Jesus. And, find the humility of Elihu, as he sought to help Job find peace in knowing the Lord. Discover practical steps to honor God in your decisions and strengthen your relationships.

Book 6 in the OBSCURE Bible Study Series follows eight interesting people in the Bible who exhibit outstanding personal attributes like courage, forgiveness, humility, and more. The book begins, however, with an example of poor character: the pride and hypocrisy of the Pharisees. The Pharisees were experts in the Jewish law, but they were more interested in following their own man-made rules and then making their compliance a matter of public record.

The second character in this study is Benaiah who on a snowy day followed a lion into a pit and killed him. Why would anyone do such a thing? What kind of courage and mental strength must one have to engage a lion in a pit? Just as one might be stunned by the courage of Benaiah, we are stunned by the lack of thankfulness of nine lepers who are healed of their terrible disease. Can you imagine being healed of such a horrible ailment and not saying, "Thank you?"

The story of Stephen reminds us to stand firm in our faith. It certainly brings to mind the question of how we would act in similar circumstances. The next subject of our study is a contrast to Stephen's standing firm. It's about Demas, who deserted Paul to pursue the values of the world. He abandoned Paul and the ministry to chase the values, pleasures, and rewards of the secular world.

The book then tackles the very challenging subject of our speech as we examine the words and actions of Rabshakeh, an Assyrian official. Speech is a very powerful tool and characteristic of the human condition. We can both heal and hurt with our words. We can both praise and slander God with our speech.

Finally the book examines Elihu, Job's young friend. Elihu waited to speak until after Job's three close friends tried to convince Job to repent for the sin in his life that must be the cause of all his problems. Job claimed to be innocent and refused to follow the advice of his friends. Elihu, in all humility waited to speak until it was obvious the friends were unsuccessful. Elihu's words and actions provide a foundation for investigating Biblical humility.

> *"Scripture holds answers in unexpected places. Our unique Bible studies reveal overlooked wisdom for today's challenges."*

The *OBSCURE* Bible Study Series – Book 6 Personal Study Guide

INTRODUCTION

We equip readers with timeless wisdom and practical tools that transform, not just inform. Our books combine deep insights with real-life application to create lasting change.

Description of The OBSCURE Bible Study Series

This unique series uses a number of lesser-known Bible characters and events to explore such major themes as Angels, being Born Again, Courage, Death, Evangelism, Faithfulness, Forgiveness, Grace, Hell, Leadership, Miracles, the Remnant, the Sabbath, Salvation, Rebellion, Sovereignty, Thankfulness, Women, the World, Creation, and End Times.

The series as a whole provides both a broad and fresh understanding of the nature of God as we see Him act in the lives of people we've never examined before.

Most of the people chosen for these studies are unfamiliar because they are mentioned only a few times in Scripture – fifteen only once or twice. Others, although more familiar, are included because of their particular contribution to kingdom work.

For example, Scripture mentions Shamgar only twice. One verse in Judges 3:31 tells his story and 5:6 simply establishes a timeline and says nothing more about him. Then there is Nicodemus, with whom we associate the concept of being "born again." His name appears only 5 times, all in one short passage in the book of John. Eve, although obviously not obscure, is included in order to investigate the creation story.

Group Discussion or Individual Study

These studies can be done individually or in a small discussion group. The real value of the study is in the discussion questions. We all see life differently and the thoughts and ideas shared in a group will often lead to a richer understanding of the Scripture. The questions often require the participant to put himself (herself) in the mind or circumstances of that person in the Scriptures.

The commentary portion of the introductory material in each lesson is there to help clarify the passage and set the stage for the discussion questions. The questions are designed to help the student understand the meaning of the text itself and explore the kingdom implications from a personal point of view.

Ideal For Both New and Mature Bible Students

These lessons have three underlying questions:

- "Who is this person?"
- "What is happening here?"
- "What is the implication for my life?"

Because of the obscurity of the characters under study, chances are that even experienced participants with prior understanding of the lesson's theme will find fresh material to explore. Both new and long-time students will be challenged by the life lessons these unfamiliar characters can teach them.

Format of Lessons

Each lesson begins with the Scripture using the ESV translation followed by short sections titled "Context," "What Do We Know," and "Observations." The discussion questions are designed to help the student understand the subject and are followed by several application questions.

"We believe applied wisdom empowers life change. Our books provide clarity, inspiration, and tools to equip readers to live their best life."

The Hypocrites
the Pharisees

> Occurrences of "hypocrites" and "hypocrisy" in the Bible: 27
>
> Themes: Hypocrisy; Pharisees, Rules

Scripture

Matthew 23:1-15, 23-33
Then Jesus said to the crowds and to his disciples, 2 "The scribes and the Pharisees sit on Moses' seat, 3 so practice and observe whatever they tell you—but not what they do. For they preach, but do not practice. 4 They tie up heavy burdens, hard to bear, and lay them on people's shoulders, but they themselves are not willing to move them with their finger. 5 They do all their deeds to be seen by others. For they make their phylacteries broad and their fringes long, 6 and they love the place of honor at feasts and the best seats in the synagogues 7 and greetings in the marketplaces and being called rabbi by others. 8 But you are not to be called rabbi, for you have one teacher, and you are all brothers. 9 And call no man your father on earth, for you have one Father, who is in heaven. 10 Neither be called instructors, for you have one instructor, the Christ. 11 The greatest among you shall be your servant. 12 Whoever exalts himself will be humbled, and whoever humbles himself will be exalted.

13 "But woe to you, scribes and Pharisees, hypocrites! For you shut the kingdom of heaven in people's faces. For you neither enter yourselves nor allow those who would enter to go in. 15 Woe to you, scribes and Pharisees, hypocrites! For you travel across sea

and land to make a single proselyte, and when he becomes a proselyte, you make him twice as much a child of hell as yourselves. . . .

23 "Woe to you, scribes and Pharisees, hypocrites! For you tithe mint and dill and cumin, and have neglected the weightier matters of the law: justice and mercy and faithfulness. These you ought to have done, without neglecting the others. 24 You blind guides, straining out a gnat and swallowing a camel!

25 "Woe to you, scribes and Pharisees, hypocrites! For you clean the outside of the cup and the plate, but inside they are full of greed and self-indulgence. 26 You blind Pharisee! First clean the inside of the cup and the plate, that the outside also may be clean.

27 "Woe to you, scribes and Pharisees, hypocrites! For you are like whitewashed tombs, which outwardly appear beautiful, but within are full of dead people's bones and all uncleanness. 28 So you also outwardly appear righteous to others, but within you are full of hypocrisy and lawlessness.

29 "Woe to you, scribes and Pharisees, hypocrites! For you build the tombs of the prophets and decorate the monuments of the righteous, 30 saying, 'If we had lived in the days of our fathers, we would not have taken part with them in shedding the blood of the prophets.' 31 Thus you witness against yourselves that you are sons of those who murdered the prophets. 32 Fill up, then, the measure of your fathers. 33 You serpents, you brood of vipers, how are you to escape being sentenced to hell?" ESV

The Context

It is interesting to note that the term "hypocrite" in its various forms occurs only once in the Old Testament. It is used frequently in the New Testament to describe the character of the Pharisees and scribes. The other Jewish leaders were no better than the Pharisees, but the Pharisees were experts in the law. Thus, they should have known what God required of His people. But rather than interpreting the law so the common man could understand it and comply, they expanded it by creating rules and requirements designed to dictate in excruciating detail every facet of daily life. These rules and regulations were unwritten interpretations passed down to each generation in oral form. Not until several hundred years after Jesus were they codified in the Mishnah (1 volume). By 500 AD they were published as the Talmud (34 volumes).

So in Jesus' day, the leaders, particularly the Pharisees, established the rules, preached the rules, and disciplined the people according to the rules. Jesus taught that compliance with laws was an attitude of the heart, not carefully following complex man made rules. However, His main criticism was that the leaders themselves did not follow their own rules.

Hypocrites!

What Do We Know?

During Jesus' ministry the word "hypocrite" was not necessarily always bad. The word actually came from theater. In this sense an actor put on a mask and pretended to be someone he was not and in the New Testament the meaning reflected this definition. But in the Gospel writings, its use is almost always in a context of evil or wrongdoing. The Pharisees pretended to be pious, told the people to be pious, but were not pious themselves.

Jesus frequently denounced the Pharisees and Jewish leaders for being hypocrites. Partly this was because they were openly opposed to Him and His teachings. His message was not consistent with what they, the Jewish authorities, were teaching the people. Jesus dealt severely with their desire to be noticed in Matthew 6. He specifically challenged their attitudes on giving to the needy, prayer, and fasting. He described them as hypocrites in each case. The Pharisees paraded their self-righteousness before the people in public displays of godliness, yet they were totally blind to the truth in God's Word.

The ultimate result was that the Jewish leaders decided they had to dispose of Jesus:

> Luke 20:19-20 *The scribes and the chief priests sought to lay hands on him at that very hour, for they perceived that he had told this parable against them, but they feared the people. 20 So they watched him and sent spies, who pretended to be sincere, that they might catch him in something he said, so as to deliver him up to the authority and jurisdiction of the governor.* ESV

Given man's fallen nature this is not surprising. Jesus was challenging the Pharisees and scribes at every turn. In our passage for this study (Mt 23), Jesus pronounced seven woes on the Pharisees and scribes. Jesus did this not in private but in front of large Jewish crowds. The Pharisees could not ignore His accusations because everyone heard what He said about them, and it wasn't good! Matthew 23 records Jesus' seven criticisms of the hypocrites:

23:13 You are shutting out the Kingdom from men, and you yourselves will not be able to enter.
23:15 You go anywhere to make a convert, then turn him into someone worse than yourself.
23:16 You make up silly rules for oaths to suit yourselves.
23:23 You tithe, but you neglect the more important matters of justice, mercy, and faithfulness.
23:25 You clean the outside of a cup but leave the inside full of greed and self-indulgence.
23:27 You are like whitewashed tombs – beautiful on outside but dead on the inside (hypocrisy and wickedness).
23:29 You claim to be more righteous than your forefathers, thus prolonging the sins of your ancestors.

Jesus ended His litany of woes with this damning accusation in 23:33, "*You serpents, you brood of vipers, how are you to escape being sentenced to hell?*" ESV

Implications and Observations

It is interesting that Jesus mentioned the Pharisees' phylacteries and fringes (Matt 23:5). Other translations call the fringes "tassels." Most of us know what a tassel is but phylacteries might be unfamiliar. They are leather boxes worn on the wrist and forehead to remind the wearer of God and His Word. The boxes, depending on size, had either one or four compartments and contained little scrolls with the following passages: Ex 13:1-10; 13:11-16; Dt 6:4-9 and Dt 11:13-21. These were worn to satisfy certain perceived requirements of the Law.

There was nothing inherently wrong with wearing these items, except that the Pharisees often wore very large leather boxes and very large tassels. Matthew records this as "they make their phylacteries broad and their fringes long." They thought these large symbols demonstrated their complete and extraordinary obedience to the Law, and thus their religious piety. This ostentatious display angered Jesus and He mentioned these two items, along with wanting places of honor at banquets, front seats at the synagogue, and being called "Rabbi" as evidence of their prideful focus on themselves.

The Pharisees practiced these behaviors to call attention to themselves and to encourage respect for their position and their religious piety. They wanted front seats at the synagogue because those seats faced the congregation. From that position they could pose and be seen with serious and holy faces by all in attendance. Jesus' point in Mt 23:8-12 is that the people need to be focused on God and God alone. We are not to elevate leaders by calling them "Father" or "Master" or even "Rabbi." We have one Father, one Lord, and one Teacher: God the Father, Jesus our Lord and Master. The leaders or greatest among us are those who humble, not exalt, themselves (23:12).

Jesus spoke of humility here because He hated pride and desired a humble spirit in His followers. Jesus' teaching is not about humility, although humility might be considered related, but about the problem of hypocrisy – saying one thing but doing another. The leaders who should have been acting in humility were instead demonstrating a spirit of pride in all they did.

Woe to You Hypocrites!

Discussion Questions

A. GENERAL

A1. If the term "Pharisee" comes up in a conversation, what do you instantly think of? What is your immediate thought about the meaning and implication?

A2. Look up in whatever source you have and list the major things that the Pharisees believed.

A3. Does what you learned in A2 above change for the better or worse your answer in A1? Explain.

A4. Carefully read Mt 23:2-3a. Jesus says to do what the Pharisees told them and to observe what the Pharisees were teaching. How does that line up with how you answered A1, A2, and A3 above?

A5. Describe what you would say were good and bad Pharisees.

    Good Pharisees: _____.

    _____.

    Bad Pharisees: _____.

    _____.

A6. Explain Mt 23:4a, "*They tie up heavy loads that are hard to carry and put them on people's shoulders.*"

A7. What is the definition of hypocrite or hypocrisy?

A8. Do you know a group, organization, or well-known person that you would call a hypocrite? How has his/her hypocrisy impacted those around him (friends, co-workers, church, general public)?

A9. Why do you think Jesus was so negative towards the Pharisees and scribes?

A10. Let's assume that the people all followed the rules and regulations of the Pharisees, regardless of whether the Pharisees followed their own rules. Would Jesus have been upset? With whom? Why? Why not?

A11. In Mt 23:24 what does Jesus mean when he says, "*You strain out a gnat but swallow a camel*"?

    Q. What are some of the little things that will cause great division in the local church?

A12. Based on this passage and your understanding, what was Jesus criticizing: the theology of the Pharisees or the Pharisees themselves?

A13. In Gal 2:11-14 Paul accused Peter of hypocrisy. What did Peter do and who was impacted?
Gal 2:11-14   *But when Cephas came to Antioch, I opposed him to his face, because he stood condemned. 12 For before certain men came from James, he was eating with the Gentiles; but when they came he drew back and separated himself, fearing the circumcision party. 13 And the rest of the Jews acted hypocritically along with him, so that even Barnabas was led astray by their hypocrisy. 14 But when I saw that their conduct was not in step with the truth of the gospel, I said to Cephas before them all, "If you, though a Jew, live like a Gentile and not like a Jew, how can you force the Gentiles to live like Jews?"* ESV

A14. Have you seen this kind of behavior in the modern church today? If yes, explain. Where could it easily occur?

.

B. RULES OF MEN

Matthew 15:2-3, 6b-9
"Why do your disciples break the tradition of the elders? For they do not wash their hands when they eat." 3 He answered them, "And

why do you break the commandment of God for the sake of your tradition? . . . So for the sake of your tradition you have made void the word of God. 7 You hypocrites! Well did Isaiah prophesy of you, when he said: 8 "This people honors me with their lips, but their heart is far from me; 9 in vain do they worship me, teaching as doctrines the commandments of men." ESV

B1. The Pharisees are being accused of revoking or nullifying God's word, which is a serious charge. What does Jesus mean here and how does that relate to the charge of hypocrisy?

B2. What rules does the church follow today that might be considered rules of men rather than rules of God? Are we teaching and requiring practices that are only the commands of men? What might those be? Possible subjects are listed below; you may think of others. What are the rules men have developed for these areas?

      a. Works.

      b. Sin and salvation.

      c. Baptism.

      d. Freedom.

      e. Sunday/Sabbath.

      f. Worship.

g. Teaching authority.

h. Communion.

i. Tithing.

j. Tattoos.

k. King James version.

l. Doctrine.

B3. In your opinion, do any of these "rules of men" nullify the doctrines or teachings of God?

B4. If we have nullified the commands of God, (1) who will be held accountable, and (2) what will be the result? If you are a disciple who has been led away from the truth by a trusted church leader, are you less accountable?

Q. What if the issue is one of salvation?

B5. How would you compare the church today with the church when Jesus was exhorting the Pharisees?

C. APPLICATION

C1. Are you a Pharisee? Do you have any Pharisaical tendencies?

C2. Do the rules of the church take priority for you over a relationship with Jesus?

C3. What spiritual rules or "doctrines" do you hold dear? Are these doctrines of God or rules of men?

C4. Do you know any whitewashed tombs (beautiful and clean on the outside, dead on the inside)?

Benaiah
killed a lion in a pit

> **Occurrences of "Benaiah"** (son of Jehoiada) **in the Bible:** 20
>
> **Themes: Courage; Loyalty**

NOTE: This Benaiah, the son of Jehoiada, chased a lion into a pit. There are at least eight other men with this same name identified in Scripture. The name "Benaiah" occurs 46 times in the Bible.

Scripture

1 Chronicles 11:22-25
<u>David puts Benaiah in charge of his bodyguard</u>

And Benaiah the son of Jehoiada was a valiant man of Kabzeel, a doer of great deeds. He struck down two heroes of Moab. He also went down and struck down a lion in a pit on a day when snow had fallen. 23 And he struck down an Egyptian, a man of great stature, five cubits tall. The Egyptian had in his hand a spear like a weaver's beam, but Benaiah went down to him with a staff and snatched the spear out of the Egyptian's hand and killed him with his own spear. 24 These things did Benaiah the son of Jehoiada and won a name beside the three mighty men. 25 He was renowned among the thirty, but he did not attain to the three. And David set him over his bodyguard. ESV

1 Kings 2:24-35
<u>Adonijah's Execution and Benaiah appointed Commander</u>
Now therefore as the Lord lives, who has established me and placed me on the throne of David my father, and who has made me a house, as he promised, Adonijah shall be put to death this day." 25

So King Solomon sent Benaiah the son of Jehoiada, and he struck him down, and he died.

26 And to Abiathar the priest the king said, "Go to Anathoth, to your estate, for you deserve death. But I will not at this time put you to death, because you carried the ark of the Lord God before David my father, and because you shared in all my father's affliction." 27 So Solomon expelled Abiathar from being priest to the Lord, thus fulfilling the word of the Lord that he had spoken concerning the house of Eli in Shiloh.

28 When the news came to Joab—for Joab had supported Adonijah although he had not supported Absalom—Joab fled to the tent of the Lord and caught hold of the horns of the altar. 29 And when it was told King Solomon, "Joab has fled to the tent of the Lord, and behold, he is beside the altar," Solomon sent Benaiah the son of Jehoiada, saying, "Go, strike him down." 30 So Benaiah came to the tent of the Lord and said to him, "The king commands, 'Come out.'" But he said, "No, I will die here." Then Benaiah brought the king word again, saying, "Thus said Joab, and thus he answered me." 31 The king replied to him, "Do as he has said, strike him down and bury him, and thus take away from me and from my father's house the guilt for the blood that Joab shed without cause.

32 The Lord will bring back his bloody deeds on his own head, because, without the knowledge of my father David, he attacked and killed with the sword two men more righteous and better than himself, Abner the son of Ner, commander of the army of Israel, and Amasa the son of Jether, commander of the army of Judah. 33 So shall their blood come back on the head of Joab and on the head of his descendants forever. But for David and for his descendants and for his house and for his throne there shall be peace from the Lord forevermore." 34 Then Benaiah the son of Jehoiada went up and struck him down and put him to death. And he was buried in his own house in the wilderness. 35 The king put Benaiah the son of Jehoiada over the army in place of Joab, and the king put Zadok the priest in the place of Abiathar. ESV

The Context:

Benaiah, Jehoiada's son, was an army officer under king David (1 Chron 18:17). He was the son of a brave man from Kabzeel, who also had a good reputation. Benaiah gained a reputation for courage and bravery as a great warrior by killing enemy warriors and by going down into a pit with a lion and killing it. He also killed a very tall Egyptian with the Egyptian's own spear.

When Adonijah tried to take Israel's throne and others committed treason, Benaiah remained loyal to king David, as did Zadok the priest, Nathan the prophet, and David's Mighty Men. After David learned of Adonijah's rebellion, he sent Zadok, Nathan, and Benaiah to crown Solomon king. After Solomon was anointed king, he sent Benaiah to kill the treasonous brother Adonijah. Benaiah also killed the defector Joab, who had been head of Israel's army, and as a result Solomon appointed Benaiah commander of the army of Israel in place of Joab.

What Do We Know?

Our focus in this study will be on 1 Chronicles 11:22-25, and in particular the fact that on a snowy day Benaiah went down into a pit to do battle with a lion. I have not researched the average weight of a lion or his running speed and leaping distance, but I'm pretty sure Benaiah was at a big disadvantage when he got to the bottom of the pit. The bigger question, of course, is why would anybody in his right mind follow a lion into a pit?

But Benaiah's exploits don't end with the lion, because the next verse says that he also killed a giant Egyptian with his own spear – a big spear, worthy of a giant. Benaiah is one scary dude! But this is just about all we really know about these events. We have very little information about the situation or circumstances surrounding these acts of bravery (some might say stupidity) that led to or caused these extraordinary events.

We know the following facts about Benaiah from 1 Chronicles 11:22-25:

- His father was Jehoiada, who was a brave man from Kabzeel.
- He killed two of Ariel's sons (Ariel was a Moabite).
- He went down in a pit on a snowy day and killed a lion.
- He killed an Egyptian giant with the Egyptian's own spear.
- He had a good reputation among the 3 warriors of David's inner circle.
- He was the most honored of David's 30 Mighty Men.
- He became David's chief bodyguard (the one in charge).

Implications and Observations

Reading the verse about Benaiah following a lion down into a pit on a snowy day almost makes us think that the story is an outrageous legend – nothing more than just folklore. But we have no reason to doubt the truth of the story. Once we get over the surprise of the unnatural idea of a man going into an open pit with a lion, then we wonder how in the world he survived. How does one get out of a pit that has a lion in it? My answer is, "very quickly!" There will obviously be a serious fight going on at the bottom of that pit and only one will come out alive.

People may look at this scene differently. Would you consider this an insurmountable problem or a great opportunity? To me it's a big problem but to a seasoned warrior living in that day it may not be as scary as I would find it. We know little about the circumstances but it does appear that Benaiah thought it was not an overwhelming problem. One might wonder what a warrior who killed a lion in a pit would do for an encore. Well, in this case he killed a giant Egyptian with the Egyptian's own weapon.

One reason David may have been drawn to Benaiah is because David himself had killed large wild animals.

> 1 Samuel 17:33-35 *And Saul said to David, "You are not able to go against this Philistine to fight with him, for you are but a youth, and he has been a man of war from his youth." 34 But David said to Saul, "Your servant used to keep sheep for his father. And when there came a lion, or a bear, and took a lamb from the flock, 35 I went after him and struck him and delivered it out of his mouth. And if he arose against me, I caught him by his beard and struck him and killed him.* ESV

It is interesting to note that David had reason to kill lions and bears. They were attacking his sheep and David was protecting the flock. Notice that David did not kill the marauders until they reared up against him. Contrasting this with the story of Benaiah, we have no information as to why Benaiah went down into a pit to kill the lion. But we have reason to believe that this event and the other acts of bravery mentioned may have led to Benaiah being part of David's Mighty Men and part of the reason Benaiah was appointed to important jobs by both David and Solomon.

Discussion Questions:

A. The LION ENCOUNTER

A1. What do we know about this lion incident?

    1) The day was _____.

    2) He went after or followed the _____ .

    3) The lion was faster and stronger than _____.

    4) The lion went into a _____ and Benaiah followed him and _____ him.

A2. List what we don't know.

A3. What is significant about it being a snowy day?

A4. What thought would go through your mind if you were in a field and came face-to-face with a lion?

> Q. Would you ever consider going into a pit after a lion? Why? Why not?

A5. What kind of courage or mental strength must exist for a man to engage a lion in a pit?

A6. Which of the following words best fit this act by Benaiah?

   Faith - Courage - Crazy - Bravery - Daring
   Fearless - Gutsy - Moxie - Insane - Bizarre?

A7. Do you think Benaiah had a Plan B when he jumped in the pit?

A8. Do we know if this was an accidental encounter or if Benaiah was tracking the lion?

A9. What was Benaiah's purpose in going into a pit containing a lion? What logical reasons can you think of for Benaiah to go down into the pit to kill a lion?

A10. Why would he go down into the pit? Wouldn't the wiser course of action have been to throw spears or shoot arrows?

A11. How would you think this act of courage may have changed Benaiah's life?

A12. Do you think this event wore on Benaiah? Might he have wondered if he could ever reproduce that level of courage again?

A13. This could have been a "defining moment" in Benaiah's life. This may have changed the path of his life. What are the defining moments in your life? What are the decisions you made or life events that changed the road on which you were traveling? [exclude marriage and the birth of children]

B. THE EGYPTIAN:

Benaiah also killed an Egyptian who was seven and a half feet tall. Even though the Egyptian had in his hand a spear like a weaver's beam, Benaiah approached him with a club, snatched the spear out of his hand, and then killed him with his own weapon.

B1. List what we know about this incident.

- The Egyptian was _____ tall.

- The Egyptian had a spear like a _____.

- Benaiah had a _____ in his hand.

- Benaiah _____ the spear from the Egyptian.

- Benaiah killed him with his own _____.

B. List what we do <u>not</u> know about this incident.

B3. This incident appears immediately following the verse about killing the lion and then 11:24 says, "*These things did Benaiah the son of Jehoiada and won a name beside the three mighty men.*" (ESV) What do you think it means that Benaiah had a reputation or "won a name" among the three mighty men?

C. RESULTS

C1. This passage tells us that Benaiah killed two Moabites, a lion, and a big Egyptian, but it tells us almost nothing about the circumstances. Why?

C2. Do you think Benaiah ever became overly confidant?

C3. The text says that, "*He was the most honored of the Thirty, but he did not become one of the Three.*" This seems strange. What might have caused Benaiah not to be part of the inner circle of Three, given he was the most honored of the Thirty?

    Q. Do you think it mattered to Benaiah?

C4. Solomon later appointed Benaiah as Commander of the Israelite Army. Why?

C5. What job did Benaiah ultimately hold under King David (1 Chronicles 11:25)?

> Q. Based on 2 Sam 23:20-23 why might David have chosen Benaiah for this position?

C6. What job did Benaiah hold under King Solomon (1 Kings 2:35)?

C7. Do you think Benaiah wanted these jobs?

D. APPLICATION

D1. Would you ever consider going into a pit after a lion, or doing anything in your life that required extraordinary courage? Explain.

D2. Is there some act of courage or bravery you need to perform?

D3. Are you one courageous decision away from changing your life? Think about it!

D4. When life gets really scary, what do you do? What is your source of comfort?

D5. Have you ever been in a group where you excelled and others recognized your special skills or abilities? How were you treated? Were you chosen to be the leader on special projects or functions?

The Ten Lepers
Jesus healed

> **Occurrences of "ten men" in the Bible:** 1
>
> **Theme:** Thankfulness

Scripture

Luke 17:11-19
Jesus Cleanses Ten Lepers

On the way to Jerusalem he was passing along between Samaria and Galilee. 12 And as he entered a village, he was met by ten lepers, who stood at a distance 13 and lifted up their voices, saying, "Jesus, Master, have mercy on us." 14 When he saw them he said to them, "Go and show yourselves to the priests." And as they went they were cleansed. 15 Then one of them, when he saw that he was healed, turned back, praising God with a loud voice; 16 and he fell on his face at Jesus' feet, giving him thanks. Now he was a Samaritan. 17 Then Jesus answered, "Were not ten cleansed? Where are the nine? 18 Was no one found to return and give praise to God except this foreigner?" 19 And he said to him, "Rise and go your way; your faith has made you well." ESV

The Context

There is no significant context in regard to the story about the ten lepers. In chapters 15-16 Luke reported some of the many parables that Jesus told His disciples. He then mentioned that Jesus was passing between Samaria and Galilee and as He entered a village He was confronted by ten lepers. It may be that this trip near Samaria triggered Luke's memory of the lepers because the one who returned to give Jesus thanks was a Samaritan. Luke then continued relating other various parables that Jesus had told them as He was traveling toward Jerusalem.

What Do We Know?

The lepers knew that Jesus had entered the village, even though they were some distance from Him. The text says they "met" him so they were probably living outside the village and saw Him coming. They referred to Him as "Master" and asked for mercy. Apparently without any other interaction, Jesus told them to go to the priest, which was required by the Law to verify that a leper was healed or "clean." Luke tells us that while the lepers were on their way to the priest, they were healed. Nothing else is said regarding the circumstances of the healing.

All ten men were healed of this terrible disease but only one returned to praise God and give thanks to Jesus. Luke then made the statement that the one returning "was a Samaritan." Remember, the Jews did not associate in any way with Samaritans:

> John 4:9 *The Samaritan woman said to him, "How is it that you, a Jew, ask for a drink from me, a woman of Samaria?" (Jews had no dealings with Samaritans.)* ESV

Jesus asked the returning leper why none of the others returned to praise God. Although it seems probable that the leper would have responded in some manner, Luke does not record a response. We do not really know the thinking or attitude of the nine lepers, except that they chose not to return and give thanks to God.

Jesus told the returning leper that his faith had made him well, implying something more than just physical healing had occurred. Nothing more is reported here concerning the ten lepers. In Matthew 8 there is a short reference to another leper, but the circumstances are significantly different. One of the major differences was that Jesus touched the one leper in Matthew 8 even though the Law prohibited such an act. Leviticus 5 says that such touching was an act of sin and required the offender to confess and make restitution in the form of an animal offering.

Implications and Observations

We have very little information regarding the circumstances surrounding the healing of the ten lepers. Although the lepers actually asked for mercy rather than healing, Jesus knew what they wanted and responded accordingly. He told them to go to the priests to be declared clean. Jesus responded immediately without asking any questions about faith, forgiveness, or anything else. He made no demands of them except to tell them to go to the priests, which they did without any other reported interaction. Going to see the priests would have been the normal procedure if one was to be declared clean or healed of the disease. The priest had to declare them clean before they could rejoin the community. This procedure is outlined in Lev 13-14.

We know there was at least one Samaritan in the group of ten, because Luke tells us that it was a Samaritan who returned to praise God and give thanks. We do not know if the one who returned was the only Samaritan or if more were Samaritans. We do know that the lepers obeyed Jesus because the author reports that all ten were healed while on their way to see the priests.

It is almost beyond belief that only one leper returned to praise God for his healing. Leprosy was a terrible disease and to be healed would have been a life-changing experience. It would have been part of the normal spiritual culture to give thanks to God for even the mundane things of life and both Samaritans and Jews were very aware of the Scriptures, particularly the Psalms, that called for giving thanks to God (see Ps 50:14; 75:1; 106:1).

Discussion Questions

A. GENERAL

A1. Describe the life of a leper in Jesus' day.

A2. If you were a leper how would you feel, think, or act?

A3. What would you have done if you were one of the lepers in this story? Why?

A4. If you were a leper today and were healed in a miraculous way, how would you feel? What would you do?

A5. Why did the ten lepers not approach Jesus?

A6. Lev 13:45ff outlines the behavior required of people with leprosy. It appears that these ten lepers did not follow all the instructions of the law. For example, they did not cry out "unclean." Do you think this is a serious breach of the Law? Does this show or indicate hearts of rebellion and disobedience? If you think it does, then why did Jesus heal them?

A7. What are the things the lepers did that we might conclude indicates they deserved healing?

A8. Why did Jesus tell the lepers to go to the priests?

A9. When did the lepers receive their healing and what are the implications?

A10. Since the lepers were not healed immediately, why do you think they were on their way to the priest?

A11. If some of the lepers were not Samaritans, the group could have been a mix of both Jew and Samaritan people. Jews and Samaritans did not associate together – Jews considered Samaritans unclean. Since it is not said otherwise, and because Scripture points out that the one who returned was a Samaritan, I believe we can reasonably assume that the group was a mix of peoples. There would have been no logic in pointing out one was a Samaritan if they were all Samaritans. What conclusions might you draw from the probability that the ten consisted of both Jews and Samaritans?

A12. How would you characterize (short descriptions) the nine that did not come back?

A13. What reasons do we have to think the nine made the wrong choice? Why did they not thank the one who healed them?

A14. What do you think spawns or creates ingratitude?

A15. How could you relate and compare this story to the nation of Israel?

A16. The returning leper's faith was demonstrated by his praise to God and falling in worship at Jesus' feet. We are left to speculate about the other lepers. Jesus told the returning leper that his faith had made him well. What, then, healed the other lepers?

A17. It would seem likely that the returning leper received something more than the others. What do you think Jesus means when He says, "*Your faith has made you well?*"

A18. How would you describe this story with regard to the requirements for salvation and particularly the difference between faith and saving faith?

A20. What does it mean to <u>you</u> to "live with an attitude of gratitude?" List three to five things:

(1). _____.

(2). _____.

(3). _____.

(4). _____.

(5). _____.

A21. How would you apply the following proverb to the story of the Ten Lepers? Do <u>you</u> think this proverb is true? Why? Why not?

"Who does not thank God for little, will not thank Him for much!"

B. APPLICATION

B1. Is there someone in your life you need to thank?

B2. What are <u>you</u> personally thankful for?

B3. Do you have an attitude of gratitude that others can see?

B4. Given your lifestyle and your Christian walk, how might you show or demonstrate gratitude to God?

B5. Psalm 103:2 says, "*My soul, praise the Lord, and do not forget all His benefits.*" Name several significant benefits that the Lord has given you, other than life, health, and salvation.

Stephen
stoned to death

Occurrences of "Stephen" in the Bible: 8

Themes: Stand firm; World's values

Scripture

Acts 6:3-15   Seven Chosen to Ensure Grecian Widows Receive Food
"Therefore, brothers, pick out from among you seven men of good repute, full of the Spirit and of wisdom, whom we will appoint to this duty. 4 But we will devote ourselves to prayer and to the ministry of the word." 5 And what they said pleased the whole gathering, and they chose Stephen, a man full of faith and of the Holy Spirit, and Philip, and Prochorus, and Nicanor, and Timon, and Parmenas, and Nicolaus, a proselyte of Antioch. 6 These they set before the apostles, and they prayed and laid their hands on them. 7 And the word of God continued to increase, and the number of the disciples multiplied greatly in Jerusalem, and a great many of the priests became obedient to the faith.

Stephen Is Seized
And Stephen, full of grace and power, was doing great wonders and signs among the people. 9 Then some of those who belonged to the synagogue of the Freedmen (as it was called), and of the Cyrenians, and of the Alexandrians, and of those from Cilicia and Asia, rose up and disputed with Stephen. 10 But they could not withstand the

wisdom and the Spirit with which he was speaking. 11 Then they secretly instigated men who said, "We have heard him speak blasphemous words against Moses and God." 12 And they stirred up the people and the elders and the scribes, and they came upon him and seized him and brought him before the council, 13 and they set up false witnesses who said, "This man never ceases to speak words against this holy place and the law, 14 for we have heard him say that this Jesus of Nazareth will destroy this place and will change the customs that Moses delivered to us." 15 And gazing at him, all who sat in the council saw that his face was like the face of an angel. ESV

<u>Acts 7:51-60</u>
"You stiff-necked people, uncircumcised in heart and ears, you always resist the Holy Spirit. As your fathers did, so do you. 52 Which of the prophets did not your father's persecute? And they killed those who announced beforehand the coming of the Righteous One, whom you have now betrayed and murdered, 53 you who received the law as delivered by angels and did not keep it."

<u>The Stoning of Stephen</u>
54 Now when they heard these things they were enraged, and they ground their teeth at him. 55 But he, full of the Holy Spirit, gazed into heaven and saw the glory of God, and Jesus standing at the right hand of God. 56 And he said, "Behold, I see the heavens opened, and the Son of Man standing at the right hand of God." 57 But they cried out with a loud voice and stopped their ears and rushed together at him. 58 Then they cast him out of the city and stoned him. And the witnesses laid down their garments at the feet of a young man named Saul. 59 And as they were stoning Stephen, he called out, "Lord Jesus, receive my spirit." 60 And falling to his knees he cried out with a loud voice, "Lord, do not hold this sin against them." And when he had said this, he fell asleep. ESV

The Context

In Acts 6 it is reported that the Grecian Jews complained that their widows were not being properly cared for and were overlooked in the distribution of food. Stephen was chosen along with six others to ensure the problem did not continue. In addition, Stephen received God's grace to perform great wonders and miraculous signs among the people which resulted in opposition from one of the Jewish synagogues. This ultimately resulted in Stephen being brought before the Sanhedrin on false charges of blasphemy.

What Do We Know?

Stephen appeared before the Sanhedrin and was asked if the charges were true. Instead of immediately answering the question, Stephen used the first 50 verses of Chapter 7 to summarize the history God's people and to point out how they had consistently rebelled and resisted His will. Then Stephen (7:51) changed from his history lesson to speak directly to the members of the Sanhedrin, calling them a "stiff-necked people" with uncircumcised hearts. Needless to say, this was not well-received.

As a result of the confrontation with the Sanhedrin, Stephen was taken out and stoned to death.

Implications and Observations

Stephen stood firm in the midst of all the false testimony that came against him. Although Stephen was not directly described as standing firm, that is exactly what he did. He held fast to his faith and like Jesus, he did not declare himself innocent of the false charges, but instead he took the offensive against the Sanhedrin's actions and accusations. When asked if the charges were true,

Stephen did not argue his innocence, but pointed out the history of the Jewish people's resistance against God.

He concluded his speech by stating that the people had even killed the prophets God had sent to Israel. The prophets had accurately predicted the coming of the Righteous One (Jesus) and now the Jews had betrayed and murdered Him. Rather than appeasing the Sanhedrin, Stephen put them on the defensive. The contrast is interesting because Stephen was described as having the face of an angel (6:15) and the Sanhedrin as being enraged (7:54).

Stephen's response was to hold fast and stand firm in his faith. Even while he was being stoned he asked the Lord not to hold this act of murder against them. Jesus made a similar request in Luke 23:34. Although not directly described as such, the message of Stephen's life was "*Stand firm*." That message is very clear in his actions, even if not stated specifically.

Therefore the questions below will focus on the challenge of standing firm, even in the face of serious consequences. In my opinion, the overriding lesson we learn from Stephen is to hold on, hold fast, and stand firm in our faith! This is the same message Jesus had for the overcomers in Revelation 2-3. Those who stood firm and overcame the obstacles of life would be highly favored and receive the rewards outlined in these two chapters in Revelation.

Are you standing firm?

The *OBSCURE* Bible Study Series – Book 6 Stephen

Discussion Questions

A. STEPHEN

A1. What do we learn about the nature and character of Stephen in the following verses?

6:5/7:55 _____.

6:8 _____.

6:15 _____.

A2. What does it mean to <u>you</u> to be "full of the Holy Spirit"? Answer in personal terms rather than theologically correct language.

A3. What would being "full of grace" mean to <u>you</u>?

A4. What did they do for Stephen in 6:6 and what does that mean?

A5. What does 6:10 mean, "*They could not withstand the wisdom and the Spirit with which he was speaking*"?

A6. When Stephen was brought before the Sanhedrin (6:11-15) to give an account of what he had been doing and saying, Stephen did not say his false accusers were lying. Did Stephen answer the high priest's question?

A7. Chapter 7:1-50 is a history lesson. It is often said that the best defense is a good offense and Stephen went on the offensive. He described how the Jews wanted to keep everything as they were and would not consider new revelation even if it came from Moses or God. What was described in Acts 7:37-43?

A8. What does Acts 7:51-53 mean?

"You stiff-necked people, uncircumcised in heart and ears, you always resist the Holy Spirit. As your fathers did, so do you. 52 Which of the prophets did not your father's persecute? And they killed those who announced beforehand the coming of the Righteous One, whom you have now betrayed and murdered, 53 you who received the law as delivered by angels and did not keep it." ESV

Q. What does "*stiff-necked people*" mean?

Q. What does "*uncircumcised hearts and ears*" mean?

Q. How would you describe "resisting the Holy Spirit"? Have you ever done that? Explain.

A9. Verse 7:56 angered the leaders to the point that they stoned Stephen. What is so damning about what Stephen said? *("Behold, I see the heavens opened, and the Son of Man standing at the right hand of God." ESV)*

A10. What would Stephen's reference to Jesus as the "Son of Man" imply to the Sanhedrin?

A11. As a summary, list the characteristics of Stephen or his life that you might want to emulate in the following verses:

6:5 _____
6:5 _____
6:8 _____
6:8 _____
6:10 _____

6:10   _____
7:51-53 _____
6:15; 7:60 _____
7:55-56 _____

B. STANDING FIRM

Following are some selected instructions from Php 1:27 – 4:1 on how to stand firm:

- 1:28   Don't be frightened by opposition to the Gospel.
- 1:29   Expect to suffer in your Christian walk.
- 2:2   Live in unity with other believers.
- 2:3, 4, 5
  -In humility, consider others better than yourself.
  -Look to the interests of others.
  -Have a selfless attitude, humility, and love for others.
- 2:12a   Obey God's commands and instructions.
- 2:12b   Work out your salvation with fear and trembling.
- 2:14   Do everything without complaining or arguing.
- 3:2   Watch out for false teachers.
- 3:3   Do not put confidence in your sinful flesh (self).
- 3:19   Do not have your minds on earthly things.

B1. Which one of the instructions above do you think would be the most difficult and why?

B2. In Php 3:19 what would you do to stand firm in this area of Christian living? Consider what radical things you might do!
Philippians 3:19   *Their end is destruction, their god is their belly, and they glory in their shame, with minds set on earthly things.* ESV

B3. Which one of the world's values do you find most difficult to ignore? Why?

B4. What happens if we don't stand firm? If we examine the train of thought for several of the key verses in the Philippians passage above, we find that the consequences of not standing firm are significant. In each of the three verses below, what is the likely or implied result of not standing firm?

The *OBSCURE* Bible Study Series – Book 6   Stephen

(1) _____.
To the Jews who had believed him, Jesus said, "If you hold to my teaching, you are really my disciples." (John 8:31 NIV)

(2) _____.
By standing firm you will gain life. (Luke 21:19 NIV)

(3) _____.
By this gospel you are saved, if you hold firmly to the word I preached to you. Otherwise, you have believed in vain.
(1 Cor 15:2 NIV)

B5. What do you think is meant by "you have believed in vain"?

B6. Does 1 Cor 15:58 help us understand the use of "in vain"?
1 Corinthians 15:58   Therefore, my beloved brothers, be steadfast, immovable, always abounding in the work of the Lord, knowing that in the Lord your labor is not in vain. ESV

B7. Paul tells his readers in Ephesians 6 to stand firm. In fact he uses the word "stand" four times in four verses. Based on Ephesians 6:11-14, how is the believer to stand firm?

Ephesians 6:11-14   *Put on the whole armor of God, that you may be able to stand against the schemes of the devil. 12 For we do not wrestle against flesh and blood, but against the rulers, against the authorities, against the cosmic powers over this present darkness, against the spiritual forces of evil in the heavenly places. 13 Therefore take up the whole armor of God, that you may be able to withstand in the evil day, and having done all, to stand firm. 14 Stand therefore . . .* ESV

Put on the full armor of God:

1) belt of _____

2) breastplate of _____

3) shoes of _____

4) shield of _____

5) helmet of _____

6) sword of the Spirit, which is the _____

7) and _____ in the Spirit.

B8. What important conclusions can you draw about standing firm from the instruction to put on the armor of God?

C. APPLICATION

C1. Are you standing firm? Do you ever waver?

C2. Is there any significant portion of the Christian doctrine that you question, are not sure you believe, or tend to ignore because you have trouble with it? What is it? (Consider talking to your small group, group leader, or pastor.)

C3. If you do not have concerns, can you be a "rock" to someone who is struggling with standing firm? Are you allowing friends or family to go unchallenged?

C4. In Question A11 we examined and listed a number of the attributes of Stephen's character and life as outlined in Acts 6:5 – 7:56. Which one of those characteristics or aspects would you like to emulate? Why?

- full of faith
- full of the Holy Spirit
- full of grace
- full of power
- wise
- speak by the Spirit
- bold
- stand firm
- not intimidated by power and authority
- see into the throne room of God

Demas
he deserted Paul

Occurrences of "Demas" in the Bible: 3

Themes: Loving the World

Scripture

2 Timothy 4:10   *For Demas, in love with this present world, has deserted me and gone to Thessalonica. . . .* ESV

Paul also listed Demas as being present with him and Luke in Colossians 4:14, and in Philemon 24 Paul named Demas as a co-worker along with several other disciples.

The Context

While imprisoned in Rome, Paul wrote this second letter to Timothy, whom he had nurtured in the faith for many years. Paul described Timothy as his co-worker in Ro 16:21 and further described his close relationship in Php 2:22, stating that Timothy had served him like a son.

Paul started the last part of this letter with heart-felt instructions to Timothy. "I solemnly charge you: proclaim the message; persist in it whether convenient or not; rebuke, correct, and encourage with great patience and teaching" (2 Tim 4:1-2). Paul followed that charge with a list of the problems Timothy was likely to encounter. He said the people would:

- not tolerate sound doctrine,
- follow their own desires,
- listen to teachers and leaders who tell them what they want to hear,
- turn away from the truth, and
- turn toward myths.

Paul then gave Timothy some personal advice: keep a clear head about everything, endure hardship, do the work of an evangelist, and fulfill your ministry. Before Paul told Timothy about Demas' desertion, he said the following about himself: I am nearing death and the time is drawing close, I have fought the good fight, I have finished the race, I have kept the faith, and I will receive a crown of righteousness.

In 4:9 Paul said, "Make every effort to come to me soon." You can almost hear the grief in his voice as he followed this plea with the news that Demas had deserted him. He finished his letter to Timothy by telling him where all his co-workers had gone. Paul asked Timothy to bring Mark with him when he came, but then warned Timothy about another co-worker, Alexander the coppersmith. Paul said that Alexander did great harm to him and that Timothy should be on guard against him because he strongly opposed Paul's preaching.

What Do We Know?

Demas had deserted Paul. "Deserted" would imply that Paul felt forsaken by Demas. He stopped helping and supporting Paul. The strong implication was that he would not return. He abandoned Paul and left him to carry on without him.

The text does not say specifically why Demas left, other than, "he loved the present world." Demas apparently decided that the values, pleasures, and rewards of the secular world were more important or more desirable than the life of a Jesus-follower. We do not know how or why this happened – we are just told it happened. It certainly appears this was a true desertion, not a situation in which Demas just decided he did not want to be in active ministry with Paul. Paul would have used different language if Demas simply decided to give up traveling with him to settle down to serve the church at Thessalonica.

"He loved this present world!"

Implications and Observations

Demas' name appears in Scripture only three times and this is the only verse that gives any information about him. The other two times merely mention his presence with Paul. We know only three important things about Demas:

(1) he deserted Paul,

(2) he loved the world, and

(3) he went to Thessalonica.

Loving the world may be one of the greatest demons in the church today! People have a "me first" mentality and it becomes easy to put the world's values ahead of godly values. Demas' departure must have been devastating to Paul. He lost a valued companion as well as fellow-missionary. Demas chose the world over Paul's friendship and a relationship with Christ. Demas may always have had one foot in the world, but at this point in his life the attraction of the world won and he left Paul. I can't help thinking that Demas sounds a lot like the younger brother in the Parable of the Prodigal Son. Both found the pull of the world irresistible.

What questions does this raise for us, especially if we are also fighting the appeal of the world? The obvious is, "What are you and I in love with?" If it's the world, our lives probably revolve around such things as money (wealth), power (influence), possessions, pleasures, or other similar pursuits. If I love something, that is what I do. We do what we love, what we value, and what we want to do.

What are you doing?

How do you spend your time? This is not a difficult question to answer, but it's one most of us don't want to think about because our choices indicate what we love. I do what I love and that's where I spend my time and resources. Demas loved the world. In John's first epistle, he identifies the source of the love we have for worldly things:

> 1 John 2:16 *For all that is in the world— the desires of the flesh and the desires of the eyes and pride in possessions— is not from the Father but is from the world.* ESV

The lust of the flesh speaks of satisfying our fleshly human desires – desires of all kinds. These lusts are only temporarily satisfying. The lust of the eyes refers to coveting the things of others and wanting them for ourselves. The pride in one's own lifestyle means we are self-focused. We really don't care about others, regardless of what we say – our actions and our inactions demonstrate we are self-absorbed.

Life is all about choices. Choices determine our walk. Choices determine our direction. Choices determine what we love! Demas apparently fell in love with the world's values. He became convinced that what the world held up as good, desirable, and commendable were the things he wanted. He was not grounded in the truth. The truth of God's Word was not determining his actions. He fell in love with what the world offered and he deserted Paul.

Nothing in this text or any other says Demas caused problems for other believers or spoke against Paul. The implication is that Demas abandoned the faith simply because he desired the values of the world over the righteousness of The Way.

Don't be a Demas!

Discussion Questions

<u>A. GENERAL</u>

A1. Put yourself in Paul's situation. How would you feel?

A2. Why did Paul tell Timothy about Demas? Did he have to tell Timothy?

A3. What positive impact do you think the news about Demas could have had on Timothy?

A4. Describe what you think it means that Demas "deserted" Paul.

A5. Paul identified five problems for Timothy (listed below). How would you compare Timothy's problems with today's church or culture?

   1) Not tolerate sound doctrine.
   2) Follow their own desires.
   3) Listen to leaders who tell them what they want to hear.
   4) Turn away from the truth.
   5) Turn toward myths.

   Q. Can you think of an example of each one of these problems in today's church?

A6. Which one of the above issues is the most prevalent today? Why?

A7. If you were in Paul's position today, giving advice to a young co-worker, what would you tell them?

A8. Today, (1) what "things of the world" might pull people away from Christ and (2) what things of the church might push people away?

A9. What happened to Demas? What might have produced this situation, other than great appeal of the "world"? Describe below how the following might have negatively influenced Demas.

PAUL:

EXCITEMENT:

FOUNDATION:

PERSECUTION:

FRIENDS:

FAMILY:

STRENGTH:

EMOTION:

A10. Do you think Paul had reason to warn the Thessalonica church that Demas was coming?

A11. If you were Paul and you saw Demas struggling, what should be your priorities? What if spending more time with Demas would negatively impact your ministry? What do you do?

B. THE WORLD

1 John 2:15-17   Do Not Love the World
Do not love the world or the things in the world. If anyone loves the world, the love of the Father is not in him. 16 For all that is in the world— the desires of the flesh and the desires of the eyes and pride in possessions—is not from the Father but is from the world. 17 And the world is passing away along with its desires, but whoever does the will of God abides forever. ESV

1 John 3:13-14   *Do not be surprised, brothers, that the world hates you. 14 We know that we have passed out of death into life, because we love the brothers. Whoever does not love abides in death.* ESV

1 John 4:4-6   *Little children, you are from God and have overcome them, for he who is in you is greater than he who is in the world. 5 They are from the world; therefore they speak from the world, and the world listens to them. 6 We are from God. Whoever knows God listens to us; whoever is not from God does not listen to us. By this we know the Spirit of truth and the spirit of error.* ESV

1 John 5:3-5   *For this is the love of God, that we keep his commandments. And his commandments are not burdensome. 4 For everyone who has been born of God overcomes the world. And*

this is the victory that has overcome the world— our faith. 5 Who is it that overcomes the world except the one who believes that Jesus is the Son of God? ESV

<u>1 John 5:19</u>   *We know that we are from God, and the whole world lies in the power of the evil one.* ESV

B1. Do you personally know anyone who quit a ministry or the church and turned to the world? What did you or they learn from that experience?

B2. If worldly values and desires were starting to become too important in your life, what would you want to happen?

B3. Why do you think God wanted a comment in the Bible about someone abandoning their faith for the world?

B4. What are some typical feelings, emotions, or sinful desires that would cause one to love the world? What do we have to guard against so as not to be entrapped by the attraction?

B5. What do you think are the two most important things that 1 John tells us about the world? Note: The word "world" occurs 187 times in the New Testament.

B6. James 4:4 tells us that friendship with the world is hostility toward God and desiring the world and its values makes us enemies of God. How would explain this to a new believer?

B7. What advice does Romans 12:2 give us in this regard?
Romans 12:2 *Do not be conformed to this world, but be transformed by the renewal of your mind, that by testing you may discern what is the will of God, what is good and acceptable and perfect.* ESV

B8. Compare Demas to the prodigal or lost son (Luke 15:1-3; 11-32). Fill in the contrasting or parallel behavior of Demas:

1. _____.
Lost son: He had been an obedient son in the past.

2. _____.
Lost son: He left home, took all he had, and he did not plan to come back.

3. _____.
Lost son: He went to another (distant) country.

4. _____.
Lost son: He squandered his wealth, spending it on wild living.

5. _____.
Lost son: No one (father or brother) went after him.

6. _____.
Lost son: He returned to his father who welcomed him home

7. _____.
Lost son: Repentant.

8. _____.
Lost son: There was a happy ending.

C. APPLICATION

C1. What do you personally love most about the world?

C2. Could anyone accuse you of loving the things of this world more than the things of God? Why?

C3. How big is the influence of the world on you?

- Q. Where do you spend your time, resources, and energy?
- Q. What do you *really* love and treasure?
- Q. What are your top two life priorities?
- Q. What would you desert your faith for?

C4. Is there someone in your life who would confront you if you began to "love the world"? Are you sure?

C5. What is the life lesson for you in this story?

Onesimus
a slave of Philemon

> **Occurrences of "Onesimus" in the Bible:** 2
>
> **Themes:** Forgiveness; Doing What is Right

Note: Only 25 verses in Paul's letter to Philemon tell us about Onesimus. In addition to the single mention of his name in this letter, Onesimus is referred to as "my child" and with approximately 10 personal pronouns throughout the letter. His name is also mentioned in Col 4:9.

Scripture   Philemon 1 – 25

<u>Greeting</u>
Paul, a prisoner for Christ Jesus, and Timothy our brother, To Philemon our beloved fellow worker 2 and Apphia our sister and Archippus our fellow soldier, and the church in your house: 3 Grace to you and peace from God our Father and the Lord Jesus Christ.

<u>Philemon's Love and Faith</u>
4 I thank my God always when I remember you in my prayers, 5 because I hear of your love and of the faith that you have toward the Lord Jesus and all the saints, 6 and I pray that the sharing of your faith may become effective for the full knowledge of every good thing that is in us for the sake of Christ. 7 For I have derived much joy and comfort from your love, my brother, because the hearts of the saints have been refreshed through you.

Paul's Plea for Onesimus

8 Accordingly, though I am bold enough in Christ to command you to do what is required, 9 yet for love's sake I prefer to appeal to you—I, Paul, an old man and now a prisoner also for Christ Jesus— 10 I appeal to you for my child, Onesimus, whose father I became in my imprisonment. 11 (Formerly he was useless to you, but now he is indeed useful to you and to me.) 12 I am sending him back to you, sending my very heart. 13 I would have been glad to keep him with me, in order that he might serve me on your behalf during my imprisonment for the gospel, 14 but I preferred to do nothing without your consent in order that your goodness might not be by compulsion but of your own free will. 15 For this perhaps is why he was parted from you for a while, that you might have him back forever, 16 no longer as a slave but more than a slave, as a beloved brother—especially to me, but how much more to you, both in the flesh and in the Lord.

17 So if you consider me your partner, receive him as you would receive me. 18 If he has wronged you at all, or owes you anything, charge that to my account. 19 I, Paul, write this with my own hand: I will repay it—to say nothing of your owing me even your own self. 20 Yes, brother, I want some benefit from you in the Lord. Refresh my heart in Christ. 21 Confident of your obedience, I write to you, knowing that you will do even more than I say. 22 At the same time, prepare a guest room for me, for I am hoping that through your prayers I will be graciously given to you.

Final Greetings

23 Epaphras, my fellow prisoner in Christ Jesus, sends greetings to you, 24 and so do Mark, Aristarchus, Demas, and Luke, my fellow workers. ESV

The Context

Onesimus appeared as the main focus in Paul's letter to Philemon. He was a runaway slave who had deserted Philemon, his owner, apparently because he stole from him. Philemon was a believer and Paul referred to him as a "co-worker" in verse 1. In verses 2-7 Paul complimented Philemon by referring to his faith and love for the church, when he said he had refreshed the hearts of his fellow believers. Paul also said that Philemon's love gave him great joy and encouragement.

It would be fair to conclude that Paul considered Philemon a good brother in Christ, as did the Christian community. Paul met Onesimus in some capacity and Onesimus became a believer (v10), so Paul wrote a personal appeal to Philemon on Onesimus' behalf.

What Do We Know?

Although Paul believed he had the right to order Philemon "to do what is required" (v8), he chose instead to request Philemon's voluntary compliance. Paul commended Onesimus as "useful to you and to me" (v11). Obviously, Paul thought highly of Onesimus.

Paul wrote for the express purpose of convincing Philemon to take Onesimus back without inflicting any serious punishment for his bad behavior. More importantly, Paul wanted Philemon to accept him as a co-worker, not as a slave. Paul's final argument was a promise to repay Philemon for any amount that Onesimus owed Philemon. This offer clearly demonstrated Paul's love and support of Onesimus.

But the fact remained that Onesimus was an escaped slave, and probably a thief as well. Paul clearly would have liked to keep Onesimus at his side, but just as clearly recognized his legal obligation to return Onesimus to his owner. According to Roman law, an owner had the right to put an escaped slave to death. So Paul did the best he could: he returned Onesimus with a heartfelt commendation and appeal to Philemon's "goodness" (v14).

Implications and Observations

Although forgiveness is a major theme of this story, Paul never actually used the word. His request was that Philemon "welcome him no longer as a slave but . . . as a dear brother" (v16). In fact, Paul wanted Philemon to welcome Onesimus back, to forgive him, and release him from slavery! It appears as Onesimus himself had to do nothing to right the situation.

It's interesting that although this letter was clearly a personal appeal to Philemon on Onesimus' behalf, Paul chose to address it to several specific individuals and the church as a whole. The letter didn't ask anything of the church, so their inclusion was either simply a courtesy or Paul wanted to use the church as leverage in order to get Philemon to abide by his requests.

It is also interesting to note that in verse 15, Paul did not say Onesimus ran away or escaped, but that Onesimus "was parted" from Philemon for a while. The entire tenor of the letter suggests that Paul probably considered Onesimus an equal rather than a slave. Although Onesimus clearly broke the law in running away and possibly stealing from Philemon, Paul's desire was for Onesimus to be accepted back as a free man and brother in Christ.

Note: Many commentaries indicate it was a common belief that Onesimus became the Bishop at Ephesus. William Barclay in his Bible Study Series tells that as the martyr Ignatious was being escorted from his church in Antioch to his execution in Rome, he wrote letters to the churches in Asia Minor. Copies of these letters still exist. In his letter to the church at Ephesus, he praised their wonderful bishop – Onesimus![1]

> **What's your opinion – is this the same Onesimus?**

Discussion Questions

A. GENERAL

A1. How did this letter get to Philemon?

A2. What was the common relationship between Paul, Philemon, and Onesimus?

A3. Why do <u>you</u> think Paul addressed this letter to the church (v2) and not just to Philemon?

A4. What was Paul doing in v4-v10?

A5. How does Paul commend Oneismus in v4-v10?

v4 I thank God for you in my _____.

v5 I have heard about your _____ in Christ, and your _____ for the saints

v6 I pray you are active in sharing your _____, and have full understanding of _____.

v7 Love encouraged me [Paul], because you have _____ ____ _____ of the saints.

v9 Paul appeals on the basis of _____.

v10 Paul describes Onesimus as his _____.

A6. On what basis did Paul appeal to Philemon in v9 and what did he mean?

A7. What did Paul mean in v10: "*my child, whom I fathered?*" Why did he use this description? What else could he have said?

A8. Find a definition of the word "onesimus" and then describe how that definition relates to v11?

A9. Given that Paul was probably in Rome and Philemon in Colossae, what was Paul doing in v12? Why?

A10. What does v13 say about how Paul compared Onesimus to Philemon?

A11. Read the text again and fill in answers to the following:

1) What did Onesimus do?

    v15 _____

    v18 _____

2) What did Paul ask Philemon to do?

v8 _____

v15-16 _____

v17 _____

v18-19 _____

A12. In v21 Paul referred to Philemon's obedience. What do you think Paul meant? What kind of relationship would call for Philemon to obey Paul in this matter?

A13. In v21 Paul also stated that he hoped that Philemon would do more than he asked. What evidence is there that Philemon did anything, let alone doing more than Paul asked?

A14. Do you think this letter sounds more like a friend writing to a friend or a mentor pressuring a disciple? Why?

A15. Let's assume that Paul was coercing Philemon. Was this appropriate on not? How do you feel about the "feel" of this letter?

A16. Is there any indication in the text that Onesimus was returning willingly to Philemon?

A17. Why would Paul go to all this trouble for Onesimus? What do you think is the overriding reason Paul took up Onesimus' cause? Why do you think Paul encouraged Onesimus to return to Philemon? Why not just let the whole thing go away? Why send Onesimus back? Why not just ask Philemon to free him?

A18. Other than returning Onesimus to Philemon, what else might Paul have done to extricate the slave from his situation?

A19. Why do you think this story is in the Bible? What would have been the result if this personal letter had not been preserved and this event had not been recorded in the canon? What important insights do you find here?

A20. If you, as a third party in this scenario, wanted to persuade Philemon to forgive Onesimus, what would be the main points of your argument?

1. _____.

2. _____.

3. _____.

B. APPLICATION

B1. List the words that Paul uses to describe Christians or believers in his letter to Philemon:

v1, 9   _____.

v1, 7, 20 _____.

v1, 24   _____.

v2   _____.

v2   _____.

v5, 7   _____.

v10   _____.

v16   _____.

v17   _____.

v23   _____.

Q. Do these words describe you? If not, why not?

B2. What do you personally learn about forgiveness from the following passages?

Matt 6:14-15   *For if you forgive others their trespasses, your heavenly Father will also forgive you, 15 but if you do not forgive others their trespasses, neither will your Father forgive your trespasses.* ESV

Matt 18:21-22   *Then Peter came up and said to him, "Lord, how often will my brother sin against me, and I forgive him? As many as seven times?" 22 Jesus said to him, "I do not say to you seven times, but seventy times seven.* ESV

Luke 23:34   *And Jesus said, "Father, forgive them, for they know not what they do." And they cast lots to divide his garments.* ESV

Q. Do you have any issues with or questions about forgiveness that you need to clarify?

B3. Is there anyone in your life you need to forgive?

B4. Is there someone in your life that you hold a grudge against because they have not asked you for forgiveness?

Rabshakeh
title of Assyrian official

Occurrences of "Rabshakeh" in the Bible: 16

Themes: Speech; Words; the Tongue

This story appears twice in the Bible, once in 2 Kings 18-19 and again in Isaiah 36-37. The title *Rabshakeh* appears eight times in each story.

Definition - Rabshakeh

Rabshakeh is a title meaning "Chief of the princes" in the Semitic Akkadian and Aramaic languages. This title was given to the chief cup-bearer or the vizier of the Akkadian, Assyrian, and Babylonian royal courts in ancient Mesopotamia.[2]

Scripture

Isaiah 36:1 – 37:8   Sennacherib Invades Judah
In the fourteenth year of King Hezekiah, Sennacherib king of Assyria came up against all the fortified cities of Judah and took them. 2 And the king of Assyria sent the Rabshakeh from Lachish to King Hezekiah at Jerusalem, with a great army. And he stood by the conduit of the upper pool on the highway to the Washer's Field. 3 And there came out to him Eliakim the son of Hilkiah, who was over the household, and Shebna the secretary, and Joah the son of Asaph, the recorder.

4 And the Rabshakeh said to them, "Say to Hezekiah, 'Thus says the great king, the king of Assyria: On what do you rest this trust of yours? 5 Do you think that mere words are strategy and power for war? In whom do you now trust, that you have rebelled against me? 6 Behold, you are trusting in Egypt, that broken reed of a staff, which will pierce the hand of any man who leans on it. Such is Pharaoh king of Egypt to all who trust in him. 7 But if you say to me, "We trust in the Lord our God," is it not he whose high places and altars Hezekiah has removed, saying to Judah and to Jerusalem, "You shall worship before this altar"? 8 Come now, make a wager with my master the king of Assyria: I will give you two thousand horses, if you are able on your part to set riders on them. 9 How then can you repulse a single captain among the least of my master's servants, when you trust in Egypt for chariots and for horsemen? 10 Moreover, is it without the Lord that I have come up against this land to destroy it? The Lord said to me, Go up against this land and destroy it.'"

11 Then Eliakim, Shebna, and Joah said to the Rabshakeh, "Please speak to your servants in Aramaic, for we understand it. Do not speak to us in the language of Judah within the hearing of the people who are on the wall." 12 But the Rabshakeh said, "Has my master sent me to speak these words to your master and to you, and not to the men sitting on the wall, who are doomed with you to eat their own dung and drink their own urine?"

13 Then the Rabshakeh stood and called out in a loud voice in the language of Judah: "Hear the words of the great king, the king of Assyria! 14 Thus says the king: 'Do not let Hezekiah deceive you, for he will not be able to deliver you. 15 Do not let Hezekiah make you trust in the Lord by saying, "The Lord will surely deliver us. This city will not be given into the hand of the king of Assyria." 16 Do not listen to Hezekiah. For thus says the king of Assyria: Make your peace with me and come out to me. Then each one of you will eat of his own vine, and each one of his own fig tree, and each one of you will drink the water of his own cistern, 17 until I come and take you away to a land like your own land, a land of grain and wine, a land of bread and vineyards. 18 Beware lest Hezekiah mislead you by saying, "The Lord will deliver us." Has any of the gods of the nations delivered his land out of the hand of the king of Assyria? 19

Where are the gods of Hamath and Arpad? Where are the gods of Sepharvaim? Have they delivered Samaria out of my hand? 20 Who among all the gods of these lands have delivered their lands out of my hand, that the Lord should deliver Jerusalem out of my hand?'"

21 But they were silent and answered him not a word, for the king's command was, "Do not answer him." 22 Then Eliakim the son of Hilkiah, who was over the household, and Shebna the secretary, and Joah the son of Asaph, the recorder, came to Hezekiah with their clothes torn, and told him the words of the Rabshakeh.

<u>Hezekiah Seeks Isaiah's Help</u>
37 As soon as King Hezekiah heard it, he tore his clothes and covered himself with sackcloth and went into the house of the Lord. 2 And he sent Eliakim, who was over the household, and Shebna the secretary, and the senior priests, covered with sackcloth, to the prophet Isaiah the son of Amoz. 3 They said to him, "Thus says Hezekiah, 'This day is a day of distress, of rebuke, and of disgrace; children have come to the point of birth, and there is no strength to bring them forth. 4 It may be that the Lord your God will hear the words of the Rabshakeh, whom his master the king of Assyria has sent to mock the living God, and will rebuke the words that the Lord your God has heard; therefore lift up your prayer for the remnant that is left.'"

5 When the servants of King Hezekiah came to Isaiah, 6 Isaiah said to them, "Say to your master, 'Thus says the Lord: Do not be afraid because of the words that you have heard, with which the young men of the king of Assyria have reviled me. 7 Behold, I will put a spirit in him, so that he shall hear a rumor and return to his own land, and I will make him fall by the sword in his own land.'" ESV

The Context:

The Northern Kingdom, Israel, was captured and taken into exile in 722 B.C. This put Judah, the Southern Kingdom, in grave danger. In fact they paid the Assyrians large sums of money to prevent an invasion. In 703 B.C. Sennacherib, the son of Assyrian's leader,

Sargon, assumed the throne of the Assyrian nation. Judah took advantage of this succession of leadership to rebel against Assyria, but after Sennacherib captured most of the other rebellious nations he came after Judah in 701 B.C. In his march on Jerusalem he captured most of the smaller Jewish cities and towns. There was not much the people could do.

When he got near Jerusalem he sent his emissary, the Rabshakeh, to meet with King Hezekiah's leaders, hoping to convince them to surrender without a fight.

What Do We Know?

We know from this passage in Isaiah that Sennacherib wanted to intimidate Hezekiah through the words delivered by the Rabshakeh. Therefore, through well-chosen words of intimidation and persuasion, the Rabshakeh attempted to convince Judah that her only course of action was to surrender.

The spoken word is extremely important. Genesis describes God's first reported release of creative energy and power was through the spoken word: "Then God said." And His last words from the Book of Revelation are: "*He who testifies about these things says, 'Yes, I am coming quickly.'* . . ." (Rev 22:20). The Bible begins and ends with a focus on the spoken word. God created man with the ability to communicate through words, and then told His Creation to testify about the Creator and His plans.

> **By the word of the LORD the heavens were made,**
> **their starry host by the breath of his mouth.** (Psalm 33:6)

Speech is essential to fellowship, relationship, and communion with God and with other human beings. We could not exist long without some form of communication. The value of the Bible depends on communication through words. If the Word of God is not exchanged or communicated, then the purpose and value of the Gospel is lost.

The Bible has much to say about words, speech, and the parts of the body we use for speech. The words "tongue," "lips," "mouth," "words," and "speech" occur nearly 1000 times in the Bible and the words "speak" and "spoke" appear another 650 times. Speech is important in the Bible! This study will look not only at the story of the *Rabshakeh* and what he had to *say*, but also at what the Bible tells us about our speech. For example, James 1:26 says, *If anyone thinks he is religious and does not bridle his tongue but deceives his heart, this person's religion is worthless.* ESV

James 3:4-10 – The Power of Speech

James 3:4-10
Look at the ships also: though they are so large and are driven by strong winds, they are guided by a very small rudder wherever the will of the pilot directs. 5 So also the tongue is a small member, yet it boasts of great things.

How great a forest is set ablaze by such a small fire! 6 And the tongue is a fire, a world of unrighteousness. The tongue is set among our members, staining the whole body, setting on fire the entire course of life, and set on fire by hell.

7 For every kind of beast and bird, of reptile and sea creature, can be tamed and has been tamed by mankind, 8 but no human being can tame the tongue. It is a restless evil, full of deadly poison. 9 With it we bless our Lord and Father, and with it we curse people who are made in the likeness of God. 10 From the same mouth come blessing and cursing. My brothers, these things ought not to be so. ESV.

After reading this passage from James one might think we would be better off if we had no tongue at all! But then the benefits of speech would also be lost. Scripture often cautions us to control the tongue, but James says that man on his own cannot tame it. However, with God's help it can certainly be put under considerable constraint. Our sinful nature will rise up from time to time and say things we regret but that does not mean we should give up. In the Day when the lion lies down with the lamb our speech will be purified, but until that Day we should do all we can to control a mouth that can so easily cause pain and heartache.

Just as the tongue has great potential for evil, so it has the ability to do good. What we do and say in our local congregations and community impacts relatively few people. But today our words can extend around the world by book, magazine, internet, TV, newspaper, and telephone, impacting people thousands of miles away. We can proclaim the Gospel in many different forms of media today compared to just 50 years ago. Our words can do great things to help establish the Kingdom.

The good _and_ bad characteristics of the tongue are described in Proverbs: *The mouth of the righteous is a fountain of life, but the mouth of the wicked conceals violence* (10:11 ESV). Unfortunately just a few ill-chosen words can destroy friendships, relationships, careers, marriages, partnerships, and families. Taking words back is not possible, and damage control often has little impact.

There is no real way to physically constrain the tongue without some form of torture. It would be easier to constrain the entire person by putting them in a soundproof room than to find a way to prevent someone from speaking. Our tongue (speech) is inordinately more powerful and more influential than its small size. Its importance and strength is out of proportion to its size.

STORY: *"Feathers In the Wind"*

Published by Bob Burg [http://www.burg.com/2009/02/feathers-in-the-wind/]

There is a 19th century folktale about a young fellow who went about town slandering the town's wise man. One day, he went to the wise man's home and asked for forgiveness. The wise man, realizing that this man had not internalized the gravity of his transgressions, told him that he would forgive him on one condition: that he go home, take a feather pillow from his house, cut it up, and scatter the feathers to the wind. After he had done so, he should then return to the wise man's house.

Though puzzled by this strange request, the young man was happy to be let off with so easy a penance. He quickly cut up the pillow, scattered the feathers, and returned to the house. "Am I now forgiven?" he asked. "Just one more thing," the wise man said. "Go now and gather up all the feathers." "But that's impossible. The wind has already scattered them." "Precisely," he answered. "And though you may truly wish to correct the evil you have done, it is as impossible to repair the damage done by your words as it is to recover the feathers. Your words are out there in the marketplace, spreading hate, even as we speak."

How interesting it is that we human beings are so quick to believe the bad that others say about someone, so accepting of the "news" contained in print and television tabloids, and so ready to assume the worst regarding another's actions, and yet we actually allow ourselves to believe that the evil we spread about someone won't really matter. It's incredible that we can't immediately and resolutely accept the fact that the gossip we speak can — and often does — do significant damage to another person.

Discussion Questions

A. THE RABSHAKEH (Isaiah 36-37)

A1. The Rabshakeh used threats and intimidation in his long speech in Isa 36:4-10. He used well-chosen words to shake the confidence of his adversaries.

36:4   What are you relying on? What are you placing your confidence in? What do you think you have?
36:5   Your plans and military preparedness are mere **empty words**.
36:5   Now that you've **rebelled**, you have no one **you can trust**.
36:6   You are trusting in Egypt, that **splintered reed of a staff**.
36:7   But you say you trust in "*the Lord our God*." Isn't He the One whose high places and **altars Hezekiah removed**.
36:8   Now let's make a deal with my master, the **king** of Assyria.
36:8   I'll give you **2,000 horses** if you can put riders on them!
36:9   How can you repel the attack of even a **single** of my master's officers, when you have to rely on Egypt for horses and chariots?
36:10 And besides, **the Lord said to me**, "*Attack this land and destroy it.*"

Q. These are very strong words. Would you be convinced by this argument?

A2. In the above speech the Rabshakeh referred at times to the king of Assyria and at other times to himself. Why do you think the Rabshakeh used this technique?

A3. What did the Rabshakeh do in Isa 36:12?
Isa 36:12   But the Rabshakeh said, "Has my master sent me to speak these words to your master and to you, and not to the men sitting on the wall, who are doomed with you to eat their own dung and drink their own urine?" ESV

A4. What did the Rabshakeh say in Isa 36:13-18 about Hezekiah?

A5. What did the Rabshakeh say about Hezekiah's God?
*Isa 36:18-20   . . . Has any of the gods of the nations **delivered** his land out of the hand of the king of Assyria? 19 **Where** are the gods of Hamath and Arpad? **Where are the gods** of Sepharvaim?*
Have they delivered *Samaria out of my hand? 20 Who among all the **gods** of these lands **have delivered** their lands out of my hand, that the Lord should deliver Jerusalem out of my hand?'" ESV*

Q. What were the Rabshakeh's tactics?

A6. Who were these other gods and why did the Rabshakeh compare the Lord with them?

A7. In Isaiah 36:21 what did the people do and why?

> Q. Why do you suppose Hezekiah told them not to respond?

A8. What did the Rabshakeh hope would happen because of his rhetoric in 36:4-19?

A9. How is Satan similar to the Rabshakeh?

B. THE TONGUE   James 3:4-10

B1. How did you react to the story about the feathers? Do you think the story is an accurate representation of what happens to our speech?

B2. What does James 3:4-10 tell us about the tongue?

3:4-5   It's power is out of _____ to its size.

3:6a   It is a _____, implying it can do both good and bad.

3:6b   It is a world of_____.

3:6c   It pollutes or stains the _____.

3:6d   It can control/impact the _____.

3:6e   It is directed by _____.

3:8a   No human being can _____ the tongue.

3:8b   It is evil full of _____ poison.

3:9-10 It can _____ (do good) and _____.(do evil)

B3. How would you argue that the tongue could "control the entire course of life"?

> Q. Do you know anyone who constantly brings calm and comfort with their speech? How would you describe their life?

> Q. Do you know anyone whose speech is constantly a burning fire? How would you describe their life?

C. WISDOM LITERATURE
(Job, Psalms, Proverbs, and Ecclesiastes)

C1. Proverbs 18:4-8 has a great deal to say about our speech:
> *4 The words of a man's mouth are deep waters;*
> *the fountain of wisdom is a bubbling brook.*

*5 It is not good to be partial to the wicked
or to deprive the righteous of justice.
6 A fool's lips walk into a fight,
and his mouth invites a beating.
7 A fool's mouth is his ruin,
and his lips are a snare to his soul.
8 The words of a whisperer are like delicious morsels;
they go down into the inner parts of the body.* ESV

Q. What do you think 18:4 means? (see also 20:5)

Q. Have you ever experienced 18:6?

Q. What does verse 18:8 mean to you?

C2. What do we learn about our speech from the following verses?

Matt 12: 37   *for by your words you will be justified, and by your words you will be condemned.* ESV

Matt 12:36 *I tell you, on the day of judgment people will give account for every careless word they speak. ESV.*

> Q. Does "every careless word" seem like an exaggeration? Is this intended to get our attention or do you think it is literally true?

> Q. James gives us further wisdom about speech in James 5:9. What does he mean?
> James 5:9   *Do not grumble against one another, brothers, so that you may not be judged; behold, the Judge is standing at the door. ESV*

C3. Compare the positive and negative characteristics of our speech in Proverbs 15:1-4:

> *1 A soft answer turns away wrath,*
> *but a harsh word stirs up anger.*
> *2 The tongue of the wise commends knowledge,*
> *but the mouths of fools pour out folly.*
> *3 The eyes of the Lord are in every place,*
> *keeping watch on the evil and the good.*
> *4 A gentle tongue is a tree of life,*
> *but perverseness in it breaks the spirit. ESV*

Q. Define "foolishness" or folly as used in 15:2.

Q. How can a "devious tongue break the spirit"? (15:4)

C4. What do the following two passages teach us?
Luke 6:45   *The good person out of the good treasure of his heart produces good, and the evil person out of his evil treasure produces evil, for out of the abundance of the heart his mouth speaks. ESV*
Matt 15:18-19   *But what comes out of the mouth proceeds from the heart, and this defiles a person. 19 For out of the heart come evil thoughts, murder, adultery, sexual immorality, theft, false witness, slander. ESV*

Q. What does the "heart" represent in the above passages?

C5. Describe the speech of the wise in the following verses.

Eccl 9:17-18   *The words of the wise heard in quiet are better than the shouting of a ruler among fools.* ESV

Eccl 10:12   *The words of a wise man's mouth win him favor, but the lips of a fool consume him.* ESV

D. EXERCISE

D1. Which words below best describe your tongue? Circle all that apply to your speech 80% of the time.

Empty	trusting	persuasive	challenging
	confident	weak	cursing

Fear	intimidating	deceiving	quiet
	misleading	slandering	gossip

Effective	soothing	powerful	accurate
	blessing	hopeful	nasty

Inspiring	mean	aggressive	strife
	gentle	healing	foolish

Angry	encouraging	comforting	gracious
	threatening	strong	untrue

Q. What did you learn from this exercise?

E. APPLICATION

E1. If <u>you</u> were mute, do you think you would tend to get into more or less trouble? Why?

E2. If you set your heart and mind to it, what and how much good could you do with your words?

E3. How difficult is it for you to remain silent? Is taming (controlling) the tongue a challenge for you?

Elihu
Job's young protagonist

> **Occurrences of "Elihu" in the Bible:** 6
>
> **Theme:** Humility

Scripture

<u>Job 32:1-16</u>   Elihu's Response
So these three men ceased to answer Job, because he was righteous in his own eyes. 2 Then Elihu the son of Barachel the Buzite, of the family of Ram, burned with anger. He burned with anger at Job because he justified himself rather than God. 3 He burned with anger also at Job's three friends because they had found no answer, although they had declared Job to be in the wrong. 4 Now Elihu had waited to speak to Job because they were older than he. 5 And when Elihu saw that there was no answer in the mouth of these three men, he burned with anger.

6 And Elihu the son of Barachel the Buzite answered and said: "I am young in years, and you are aged; therefore I was timid and afraid to declare my opinion to you. 7 I said, 'Let days speak, and many years teach wisdom.' 8 But it is the spirit in man, the breath of the Almighty, that makes him understand. 9 It is not the old who are wise, nor the aged who understand what is right. 10 Therefore I say, 'Listen to me; let me also declare my opinion.'

11 "Behold, I waited for your words, I listened for your wise sayings, while you searched out what to say. 12 I gave you my attention, and, behold, there was none among you who refuted Job or who answered his words. 13 Beware lest you say, 'We have found wisdom; God may vanquish him, not a man.' 14 He has not directed his words against me, and I will not answer him with your speeches.

15 "They are dismayed; they answer no more; they have not a word to say. 16 And shall I wait, because they do not speak, because they stand there, and answer no more? ESV

Context

Job was introduced in Chapter 1 as a man of integrity who feared God and turned away from evil. Through a series of circumstances Job incurred hard times: he lost his family, his servants, and much of his wealth. He also became infected with terrible boils all over his body. His wife suggested that he curse God and die, but Job answered:

> Job 2:10   But he said to her, "You speak as one of the foolish women would speak. Shall we receive good from God, and shall we not receive evil?" In all this Job did not sin with his lips. ESV

At that point three friends arrived to comfort Job and from there through chapter 31 the focus is on their advice. They claimed that Job's suffering was because of his sin. Job protested that he had not sinned and even demanded that God personally confront him. Job wanted justice! The arguments came to a standstill when a fourth friend entered the fray: Elihu.

Biblical Humility

In this short passage Elihu demonstrated characteristics of humility. Jesus Himself best demonstrated this character trait but there are a number of other examples in Scripture:

1) Moses – Numbers 12:3
Now the man Moses was very meek, more than all people who were on the face of the earth. ESV

2) Josiah – 2 Chronicles 34:27
because your heart was tender and you humbled yourself before God when you heard his words against this place and its inhabitants, and you have humbled yourself before me and have torn your clothes and wept before me, I also have heard you, declares the Lord. ESV

3) Ahab – 1 Kings 21:29
Have you seen how Ahab has humbled himself before me? Because he has humbled himself before me, I will not bring the disaster in his days; but in his son's days I will bring the disaster upon his house." ESV

Q. List some other biblical characters who exhibited humility.

1.

2.

3.

Christ's Humility

HUMILITY DESCRIBED:

Php 2:3-8 *Do nothing from rivalry or conceit, but in humility count others more significant than yourselves. 4 Let each of you look not only to his own interests, but also to the interests of others. 5 Have this mind among yourselves, which is yours in Christ Jesus, 6 who, though he was in the form of God, did not count equality with God a thing to be grasped, 7 but made himself nothing, taking the form of a servant, being born in the likeness of men. 8 And being found in human form, he humbled himself by becoming obedient to the point of death, even death on a cross.* ESV

Q. What does it mean to "*count others more significant than yourselves*"? What are some acts that would illustrate this?

    MEANING:

    ACTS:

HUMILITY DEMONSTRATED:

John 13:3-5, 14-15
Jesus, knowing that the Father had given all things into his hands, and that he had come from God and was going back to God, 4 rose from supper. He laid aside his outer garments, and taking a towel, tied it around his waist. 5 Then he poured water into a basin and began to wash the disciples' feet and to wipe them with the towel that was wrapped around him. . . . 14 If I then, your Lord and Teacher, have washed your feet, you also ought to wash one another's feet. 15 For I have given you an example, that you also should do just as I have done to you. ESV

Q. What was Jesus teaching His disciples in John 13:1-17?

Q. Choose one of the above passages and describe how humility is demonstrated and what that act of humility means to you.

HOW DEMONSTRATED:

MEANING:

Pride Comes Before the Fall

The story is told of two ducks and a frog who lived happily together in a farm pond. The best of friends, the three would amuse themselves and play together in their waterhole. When the hot summer days came, however, the pond began to dry up, and soon it was evident they would have to move. This was no problem for the ducks, who could easily fly to another pond. But the frog was stuck. So it was decided that they would put a stick in the bill of each duck that the frog could hang onto with his mouth as they flew to another pond. The plan worked well – so well, in fact, that as they were flying along a farmer looked up in admiration and mused, "Well, isn't that a clever idea! I wonder who thought of it?" The frog said, "I did" . . . . *SPLAT!* [3]

Q. Have you ever done anything like this?

Humility in Action

A truly humble man is hard to find, yet God delights to honor such selfless people. Booker T. Washington, the renowned African-American educator, was an outstanding example of this truth. Shortly after he took over the presidency of Tuskegee Institute in Alabama, he was walking in an exclusive section of town when he was stopped by a wealthy white woman. Not knowing the famous Mr. Washington by sight, she asked if he would like to earn a few dollars by chopping wood for her. Because he had no pressing business at the moment, Professor Washington smiled, rolled up his sleeves, and proceeded to do the humble chore she had requested. When he was finished, he carried the logs into the house and stacked them by the fireplace. A little girl recognized him and later revealed his identity to the lady.

The next morning the embarrassed woman went to see Mr. Washington in his office at the Institute and apologized profusely. "It's perfectly all right, Madam," he replied. "Occasionally I enjoy a little manual labor. Besides, it's always a delight to do something for a friend." She shook his hand warmly and assured him that his meek and gracious attitude had endeared him and his work to her heart. Not long afterward she showed her admiration by persuading some wealthy acquaintances to join her in donating thousands of dollars to the Tuskegee Institute.[4]

Q. What was wrong with the woman's request?

Q. What would you have done under the same circumstances?

Q. Why do you think that Mr. Washington chopped the wood?

Discussion Questions

A. ELIHU:

A1. In general, why might Elihu have decided to speak?

A2. Based on Job 32:2-3 why was Elihu angry?
Then Elihu the son of Barachel the Buzite, of the family of Ram, burned with anger. He burned with anger at Job because he justified himself rather than God. 3 He burned with anger also at Job's three friends because they had found no answer, although they had declared Job to be in the wrong. ESV

WITH JOB:

WITH FRIENDS:

Q. Elihu's response is in chapters 32-37. What might we conclude, without reading the text about what Elihu had to say?

A3. Job 32:4 says that Elihu waited to speak. Why?

A4. What might have happened if Elihu had spoken first or inserted himself into the conversation earlier?

A5. Job 32:5 says that Elihu became angry. Why?

A6. What was Elihu saying in 32:6-10?

ABOUT BEING YOUNG:

Q. Do you think this is true today?

ABOUT BEING OLD:

ABOUT WISDOM/UNDERSTANDING:

A7. What did Elihu do in 32:11-12?

Q. Specifically what does Elihu say he did?

A8. Based on 32:1-16 how would you describe Elihu? What kind of person was he? <u>Underline</u> or highlight below the words or phrases that describe Elihu's character.

<u>Job 32:1-16</u>
*So these three men quit answering Job, because he was righteous in his own eyes. 2 Then **Elihu** son of Barachel the Buzite from the family of Ram became angry. He was angry at Job because he had justified himself rather than God. 3 He was also angry at Job's three friends because they had failed to refute him, and yet had condemned him. 4 Now **Elihu** had waited to speak to Job because they were all older than he. 5 But when he saw that the three men could not answer Job, he became angry. 6 So **Elihu** son of Barachel the Buzite replied: I am young in years, while you are old; therefore I was timid and afraid to tell you what I know.*

7 I thought that age should speak and maturity should teach wisdom. 8 But it is a spirit in man and the breath of the Almighty that give him understanding. 9 It is not only the old who are wise or the elderly who understand how to judge. 10 Therefore I say, "Listen to me. I too will declare what I know."

11 Look, I waited for your conclusions; I listened to your insights as you sought for words. 12 I paid close attention to you. Yet no one proved Job wrong; not one of you refuted his arguments.13 So do not claim, "We have found wisdom; let God deal with him, not man.". . . Job's friends are dismayed and can no longer answer; words have left them. 16 Should I continue to wait now that they are silent, now that they stand there and no longer answer? HCSB

Q. Summarize Elihu's character or attributes:

A9. If you were Job, would you have listened to Elihu? Explain.

B. HUMILITY

B1. List words or phrases describing how a truly humble person might act.

1.

2.

3.

4.

B2. Who is the best example you can think of (outside of the Bible) of someone living a life of humility?

C. LUKE 18:9-14

The Pharisee and the Tax Collector
He also told this parable to some who trusted in themselves that they were righteous, and treated others with contempt: 10 "Two men went up into the temple to pray, one a Pharisee and the other a tax collector. 11 The Pharisee, standing by himself, prayed thus:

'God, I thank you that I am not like other men, extortioners, unjust, adulterers, or even like this tax collector. 12 I fast twice a week; I give tithes of all that I get.' 13 But the tax collector, standing far off, would not even lift up his eyes to heaven, but beat his breast, saying, 'God, be merciful to me, a sinner!' 14 I tell you, this man went down to his house justified, rather than the other. For everyone who exalts himself will be humbled, but the one who humbles himself will be exalted." ESV

C1. What is wrong with what the Pharisee did?

C2. What Old Testament passage would you recommend the Pharisee read?

C3. What did the tax collector do that would have pleased Jesus?

D. APPLICATION

D1. How important is humility to you in your relationships?

D2. What is the most humble thing you have ever done? Who noticed?

D3. If you were going to do <u>one</u> thing on a regular basis to practice humility or to be more humble, what would it be? Why?

D4. The tax-collector said, *"God, have mercy on me, a sinner."* Have you ever said that?

The *OBSCURE* Bible Study Series – Book 6

Transformation Road Map
Primary Takeaways

1: True righteousness comes from a humble heart focused on God, not from outward displays of piety or adherence to man-made rules.

2: Unwavering courage and trust in God can lead to extraordinary victories, even in the face of seemingly insurmountable challenges.

3: Gratitude and worship are essential responses to God's grace, as true faith recognizes and honors the Giver, not just the gift.

4: We are called to stand firm in our faith, boldly proclaim the truth, and extend forgiveness, even in the face of persecution or death.

5: Loving the world over God leads to spiritual failure, demonstrating the need to remain steadfast in faith and prioritize eternal values over temporary pleasures.

6: The transformative power of Christ's love and forgiveness can radically change lives, elevating former sinners to beloved brothers and sisters in the faith, regardless of their past or social status.

7: Our words have immense power to either build up or tear down, highlighting the critical importance of using our speech wisely and in alignment with God's truth, especially in the face of intimidation or opposition.

8: True wisdom and understanding come from humility before God and reliance on His Spirit, not merely from age or human experience.

The *OBSCURE* Bible Study Series – Book 6

Free PDF
MAKE WISE DECISIONS

[Get the ebook version for 99 cents]

Consequences Shape Lives.

This book discusses the nature of decisions and explores eight essential questions to make better decisions.

You are a few decisions away from transforming your life. You can make better decisions! This resource has sections on what makes a poor decision, questions to ask yourself, traps to avoid, short and sweet decisions, the wise decision framework, and twenty ways to be wise. It also has a handy decision-making checklist. (12 pages)

Free PDF: https://getwisdompublishing.com/resource-registration/

Kindle ebook for 99 cents: https://www.amazon.com/dp/B0FG8NC53J

Ebook

Free PDF

Ten Steps to Wise Choices

Timeless Wisdom. Practical Tools. Lasting Impact.

The *OBSCURE* Bible Study Series – Book 6

Free PDF
Life Improvement Principles
[Get the ebook version for 99 cents]

You can live your best life!

Welcome to a journey of discovery! In case you have forgotten, your actions have consequences. Unlock your potential! This book (60+ pages) provides the overview of all our strategies and wisdom principles to live your best life. You *can* transform your life! Get your wisdom-based roadmap to a better life and unlock all the possibilities for growth and success.

Free PDF: https://getwisdompublishing.com/resource-registration/

Kindle ebook for 99 cents:
https://www.amazon.com/dp/B0FG883KZM

Ebook

Free PDF

Make it your life goal to be the best you can be!

Discover Wisdom and live the life you deserve.

The *OBSCURE* Bible Study Series – Book 6

Next Steps!

Continue Studying the *OBSCURE* Series
The *OBSCURE* Bible Study Series
https://www.amazon.com/dp/B08T7TL1B1

Be Challenged by the Jesus Follower Series
The Jesus Follower Bible Study Series
https://www.amazon.com/dp/B0DHP39P5J

Tackle Wisdom-Driven Life Change
Apply Biblical Wisdom to Live Your Best Life!
"Effective Life Change"
https://www.amazon.com/dp/1952359732

Know What You Should Pray
Personal Daily Prayer Guide
https://www.amazon.com/What-Should-Pray-Personal-Journal/dp/1952359260/

Decide to be the Very Best You Can Be
The Life Planning Series
https://www.amazon.com/dp/B09TH9SYC4

You Can Help:
SOCIAL MEDIA: Mention The *OBSCURE* Bible Study Series on your social platforms. Include the hashtag #obscurebiblestudy so we are aware of your post.

FRIENDS: Recommend *OBSCURE* to your family, friends, small group, Sunday School class leaders, or your church.

REVIEW: Please give us your honest review at
https://www.amazon.com/dp/1952359120

The *OBSCURE* Bible Study Series

Continue your journey through the hidden
wisdom of Scripture with the OBSCURE Series.

  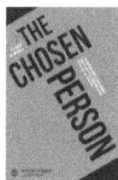 

Blasphemy, Grace, Quarrels & Reconciliation: The lives of first-century disciples.
This book presents Joseph of Arimathea, Joanna, Ananias, Hymenaeus, and Cornelius (a centurion). It illustrates the nature and challenges of life as a first-century disciple.

The Beginning and the End: From creation to eternity.
This book has four lessons from Genesis and four from Revelation covering creation, rebellion, grace, worship, and eternity. God is leading us to worship in the Throne Room.

God at the Center: He is sovereign and I am not.
This book examines the virgin birth, worship, prayer, the sovereignty of God, compromise, and trust. God is at the center of all these stories. He is at the center of our lives.

Women of Courage: God did some serious business with these women.
This book examines the lives of Jael, Rizpah, the woman of Tekoa, Tabitha, Shiphrah, and Lydia. These women exhibit great courage and faithfulness. God used them in amazing ways.

The Beginning of Wisdom: Your personal character counts.
In this book we find courage, loyalty, thankfulness, love, forgiveness, and humility. Personal character counts. Decisions have consequences. Wisdom will help us stand firm in our faith.

Miracles & Rebellion: The good, the bad, and the indifferent.
God hates sin and loves to heal the faithful. The rebellion of Korah, Haman, and Alexander compare to the healing stories of Aeneas, a slave girl, and the crippled man at Lystra.

The Chosen People: There is a remnant.
This book concentrates mostly on Israel in the Old Testament, but also covers some interesting subjects as Lucifer, Michael the archangel, and Job's wife.

The Chosen Person: Keep your eyes on Jesus.
The focus is on Jesus and the superiority of Christ. We investigate Melchizedek, the disciples on the road to Emmaus, Nicodemus, and the criminal on the cross.

WEBSITE: http://getwisdompublishing.com/products/
AMAZON: www.amazon.com/author/stephenhberkey

The *OBSCURE* Bible Study Series – Book 6

Jesus Follower Bible Study Series

The Jesus Follower Bible Study Series will provide you with a complete description of the nature, characteristics, obligations, commitments, and responsibilities of a true Jesus follower.

Go to our Amazon Book Series page for your copy:
https://www.amazon.com/dp/B0DHP39P5J

The RELATIONSHIP CHARACTERISTICS of a Jesus Follower:
    Are you right with God?
The ONE ANOTHER INSTRUCTIONS to a Jesus Follower:
    Are you right with one another?
The WORSHIP of a Jesus Follower:
    Is your worship acceptable or in vain?
The PRAYER of a Jesus Follower:
    What Scripture says about unleashing the power of God.
The DANGERS of SIN for a Jesus Follower:
    God HATES sin! He abhors sin!
The FOCUS for a Jesus Follower:
    Keep your eyes fixed on Jesus!
The HEART Requirements of a Jesus Follower:
    Follow with all your heart, mind, body, and soul!
The COMMITMENTS of a Jesus Follower:
    Practical Christian living and discipleship.
The OBEDIENCE Requirements for a Jesus Follower:
    Ignore at your own risk!

"Get Wisdom Publishing creates wisdom-driven products that equip readers with timeless insights, understanding, and actionable tools to transform their lives."

The *OBSCURE* Bible Study Series – Book 6

Life Planning Series

Read these books if you want to live a better life.
The primary audience for this series is the secular self-help market, but the concepts are Christian based.

	For the spiritual seeker and those with spiritual questions. *Your Spiritual Guidebook For Questions About Religion, God, Heaven, Truth, Evil, and the Afterlife.* https://www.amazon.com/dp/1952359473
	Core values will drive your life. https://www.amazon.com/dp/195235949X

Other Titles in the Life Planning Series
CHOOSE Integrity
CHOOSE Friends Wisely
CHOOSE The Right Words
CHOOSE Good Work Habits
CHOOSE Financial Responsibility
CHOOSE A Positive Self-Image
CHOOSE Leadership
CHOOSE Love and Family
LIFE PLANNING HANDBOOK A Life Plan Is The Key To Personal Growth https://www.amazon.com/gp/product/1952359325

Go to:

https://www.amazon.com/dp/B09TH9SYC4

to get these books.

The *OBSCURE* Bible Study Series – Book 6

Personal Daily Prayer Guide
Prayer Resource and Journal

This is a great resource to kick-start your prayer life!

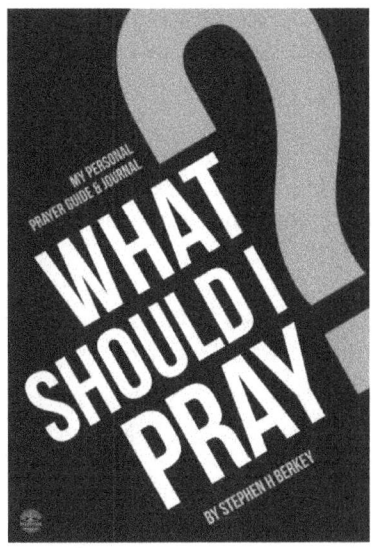

Know what to pray.
Pray based on Bible verses.
Strengthen your prayer life.
Access reference resources.
Pray with eternal implications.
Write your own prayers if desired.
Organize and focus your prayer time.
Learn what the Bible says about prayer.
Find encouragement and advice on how to pray.
Reduce frustration and distraction in your prayer time.

Get your copy today!

https://www.amazon.com/What-Should-Pray-Personal-Journal/dp/1952359260/

Acknowledgments

Arlene
Arlene has served as wife, editor, and proof-reader for all of my writing – thank you for your patience, help, and love.

Michelle
Michelle, our older daughter, has been an invaluable resource. She has graciously produced the website at www.getwisdompublishing.com. She was the first author in the family: graceandthegravelroad.com.

Stephanie
Our middle daughter designed all the covers for the *OBSCURE* Bible Study Series, as well as the marks and logos for Get Wisdom Publishing. We are grateful for her talent!

KOINONIA Small Group
These dear friends have hung in there with me as I taught many of the lessons to them first. Their input, answers, and suggestions have been invaluable.

God, Jesus, and Holy Spirit
Thank you, Lord, for Your guidance and direction.

The *OBSCURE* Bible Study Series – Book 6

Notes

1 The NIV Study Bible, New International Version, Zondervan Publishing House, © 1985, study notes in Matthew 23 on what the Pharisees believed.

2 HCSB Study Bible, Holman Christian Standard Bible, Holman Bible Publishers, Nashville TN, © 2010, study notes on Matthew 23:2-3.

3 Nelson's Illustrated Bible Dictionary, Copyright © 1986, Thomas Nelson Publishers; from PC Study Bible, "Leper"

4 Nelson's Illustrated Bible Dictionary, Copyright © 1986, Thomas Nelson Publishers; from PC Study Bible, "Master"

5 Nelson's Illustrated Bible Dictionary, Copyright © 1986, Thomas Nelson Publishers; from PC Study Bible, "stiff-necked"

6 Nelson's Illustrated Bible Dictionary, Copyright © 1986, Thomas Nelson Publishers; from PC Study Bible, "circumcision" and "uncircumcised hearts"

7 *The Letters to Timothy, Titus and Philemon,* in The Daily Study Bible Series, edited by William Barclay; The Westminster Press, Philadelphia, ISBN 0-664-20330-2.

8 Wikipedia, the Free Encyclopedia, https://en.wikipedia.org/wiki/Rabshakeh.

9 Nelson's Illustrated Bible Dictionary, Copyright © 1986, Thomas Nelson Publishers; from PC Study Bible, "Foolish"

10 *Today in the Word*, April, 1989, p. 34.

11. http://www.sermonillustrations.com/a-z/humility.htm

About the Author

Steve attended church as a child and accepted Christ when he was 10 years old. But his walk with Jesus left a lot to be desired for the next 44 years. In 1994 he "wrestled" with God for some period of months and in September of that year totally surrendered his life to Jesus.

In 1996 he was so driven to study God's Word that he attended the Indianapolis campus of Trinity Evangelical Divinity School (Chicago) to earn a Certificate of Biblical Studies. His hunger for God's Word led him to lead and write all his own Bible studies for his small group. He has been an entrepreneur and Bible study leader for the past 30 years.

He is a member of The Church at Station Hill in Spring Hill, TN, a regional campus of Brentwood Baptist (Brentwood TN).

www.getwisdompublishing.com

"Get Wisdom Publishing is dedicated to being the trusted source of wisdom-driven books that inspire growth, guide decisions, and empower readers to live with purpose and fulfillment."

The *OBSCURE* Bible Study Series – Book 6

Contact Us

Website: www.getwisdompublishing.com

Email: info@getwisdompublishing.com

Facebook: Get Wisdom Publishing

Author's Page: www.amazon.com/author/stephenhberkey

Amazon's Obscure Bible Study Series page:
https://www.amazon.com/dp/B08T7TL1B1

"Go beyond devotionals.
Experience biblical wisdom in action!"

www.ingramcontent.com/pod-product-compliance
Lightning Source LLC
Chambersburg PA
CBHW061329040426
42444CB00011B/2836